China's Maritime Silk Road
and Asia

China's Maritime Silk Road and Asia

Editors
Vijay Sakhuja
Jane Chan

National
Maritime
Foundation

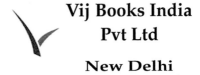

**Vij Books India
Pvt Ltd**

New Delhi

Published by

Vij Books India Pvt Ltd
(Publishers, Distributors & Importers)
2/19, Ansari Road
Delhi – 110 002
Phones: 91-11-43596460, 91-11-47340674
Fax: 91-11-47340674
e-mail: vijbooks@rediffmail.com
we b: www.vijbooks.com

First Published : 2016

ISBN: 978-93-84464-98-1 (Hardback)

ISBN: 978-93-85563-12-6 (ebook)

Price in India : ₹ 695/-

The views expressed in this book are those of the contributors in their personal capacity. These do not have any institutional endorsement.

Printed and bound in India

Contents

Contributors   vii

Foreword   ix

Abbreviations   xi

Introduction   xiii

1. Geopolitics of China's 'Maritime Silk Road' Concept:
   An Indian Perspective   1

   Gurpreet S Khurana

2. China's 'One Belt, One Road' Initiative: The Convergence
   of Strategic Interests and Domestic Imperatives   14

   Mingjiang Li

3. Security Dimension of China's 21st Century Maritime
   Silk Road : Indian Ocean Context   23

   Raghavendra Mishra

4. Southeast Asian Responses to China's 21st Century
   Maritime Silk Road Initiative   47

   Irene Chan, Associate

5. The 21st Century Maritime Silk Road: The Beijing
   Consensus Revisited from a South Asian Perspective   66

   Rana Divyank Chaudhary

6. China's Africa Push for Maritime Silk Road   80

   Antara Ghosal Singh

7. The Idea of a Maritime Silk Road: History of an Idea   99

    Kwa Chong Guan

8. Revisiting Maritime Past: Maritime Silk Road and
    Project Mausam   111

    Adwita Rai

Appendix - ***Vision and Actions on Jointly Building***   125
            Silk Road Economic Belt and 21st-Century
            Maritime Silk Road - National Development
            and Reform Commission, Ministries of Foreign
            Affairs and Commerce, People's Republic of China,
            with State Council authorization,   28 March 2015

Index   143

Contributors

Ms. Adwita Rai, Research Associate at the National Maritime Foundation (NMF), New Delhi.

Ms. Antara Ghosal Singh, Research Associate at the National Maritime Foundation (NMF), New Delhi.

Captain Gurpreet S Khurana, Executive Director of the National Maritime Foundation (NMF), New Delhi

Ms. Irene Chan, Associate Research Fellow at the Rajaratanam School of International Studies, Singapore.

Mr. Kwa Chong Guan, Senior Fellow at the Rajaratanam School of International Studies, Singapore.

Dr. Mingjiang Li, Associate Professor at the Rajaratanam School of International Studies, Singapore.

Captain Raghavendra Mishra, Research Fellow at the National Maritime Foundation (NMF), New Delhi

Mr. Rana Divyank Chaudhary, Research Associate at the National Maritime Foundation (NMF), New Delhi.

Foreword

The rise of China is an issue of animated discussion, evident from the large volume of analytical and scholarly work being devoted to its study. Any policy declaration emanating from China invites, 'a wide array' of comments and analyses of cooperative, competitive and conflictual nature, based on one's personal or theoretical persuasion. This is also the case with regard to the 'One Belt One Road' (OBOR) initiative by China. The OBOR initiative runs along two axes – one each terrestrial and oceanic, i.e., the Silk Road Economic Belt (SREB) and the 21st Century Maritime Silk Road (MSR). The OBOR connects China and the Europe passing through Eurasia, the Indian Ocean littorals, including Africa.

It is also worth mention that both the Silk Roads have multiple nodes, tributaries and spokes that feed into these transcontinental initiatives. Both initiatives are rooted in history as the point of reference and founded on the common pillars of economic integration, infrastructure development, regional connectivity, with enhanced people-to-people contact, as the logical policy byproducts.

There are many prisms through which the MSR can be analyzed; it can be stated that it presents unique opportunities and challenges simultaneously. While beneficial aspects are important, and need to be taken forward to their logical ends, the issue of dealing with some harsh realities cannot be lost sight of. Perhaps, it is important to create a 'delicate balance' between the 'give and take' on this complex issue which spans countries, sub-regions and regions that are expected to form part of the MSR, including the world as a whole.

The existing narrative on MSR also raises some important questions - is it correct to ascribe excessive Sino centricity to the Silk Road concepts; do all roads, routes, and offshoots lead to China; and, whether these will actually be under the exclusive control of Beijing. There are no easy answers to these questions at this stage.

This edited volume comprises papers presented during the interaction between the National Maritime Foundation (NMF), New Delhi and the Rajaratnam School of International Studies (RSIS) Singapore and captures the flavor of the times and could serve as a point of departure for the emerging discourse on the issue. Further, the perspectives presented here would help in understanding the conceptual tenets of the MSR initiative and provide a good reference point to take the research forward on this topic.

Admiral DK Joshi
PVSM, AVSM, YSM, NM, VSM (Retd)
Chairman National Maritime Foundation
Former Chief of the Naval Staff

New Delhi

Abbreviations

ADIZ	Air Defence Identification Zone
AIIB	Asian Infrastructure Investment Bank
ASBM	Anti-Ship Ballistic Missile
ASEAN	Association of South East Asian Nations
BCIM	Bangladesh-China-India-Myanmar
BFA	Boao Forum For Asia
BRI	Belt Road Initiative
CNPC	China National Petroleum Corporation
CPEC	China-Pakistan Economic Corridor
CUES	Conduct On Unelated Encounters As Sea
DIPP	Department of Industrial Policy and Promotion
EAS	East Asia Summit
ECS	East China Sea
FGP	Flying Geese Paradigm
GMS	Greater Mekong River Sub-Region
IOR	Indian Ocean Region
MoU	Memorandum of Understanding
MSR	Maritime Silk Road
NDRC	National Development and Reform Commission
NDU	National Defence University
OBOR	One Belt One Road
ONGC	Oil and Natural Gas Corporation
PLAN	People Liberation Army (Navy)
SCO	Shanghai Cooperation Organization
SCS	South China Sea

SIPRI	Stockholm International Peace Research Institute
SREB	Silk Road Economic Belt
TAZARA	Tanzania Zambia Railway
TIV	Trend Indicator Value
TPP	Trans-Pacific-Partnership
USD	US Dollar
WPNS	Westerns Pacific Naval Symposium

Introduction

Chinese President Xi Jinping's proposals in 2013 of the Silk Road Economic Belt (SREB) and the 21st Century Maritime Silk Road (MSR), now known as the 'One Belt, One Road' Initiative (OBOR), have drawn much attention in Asia and beyond. This volume focus only on the 21st Century MSR, seeking to better understand the rationale behind the Chinese proposal, what the initiative actually entails, and what are some of the foreseeable economic, security and strategic implications for Asia.

In the first Chapter, Captain Khurana posits that the Chinese leadership has developed the acumen for combining 'symbolism' and 'realism' to meet China's national objectives. The MSR concept is an apt example of such a skill, and may well be considered a representation of evolving Chinese statecraft since the era of Mao Zedong. This chapter, examines various nuances of the MSR in the context of China's likely grand-strategic objectives in the Indo-Pacific region, and avers that even as the concept is showcased by China as an 'initiative' with a purely 'economic' agenda, it bears a strong 'geopolitical' context and content, with far-reaching ramifications for the region.

Li Mingjiang in Chapter Two explains that the contemporary narrative of the MSR and emphasizes that as part of the Belt Road Initiative (BRI), it should be understood as a Chinese grand Strategy adopted under the leadership of President Xi. Whilst the most common criticism of the initiative - the lack of a concrete implementation plan, is true; Li argues that Beijing is inclined to push through regardless of the obstacles it may face. Obstacles illustrated in the chapter range from domestic scepticism to the lukewarm support from external partners. This is despite the fact that Southeast Asian countries and China are enmeshed in a web of bilateral and multilateral engagements, and China is their largest trading partner.

In Chapter Three, Captain Mishra avers that 'security connotations' of MSR cannot be examined from a traditional politico-military perspective.

In a globalized but somewhat uncertain international environment, the three "geos" of geography, geopolitics and geo-strategy would need to factor aspects of geo-economics and resource flow patterns. Further, a more holistic analysis of the China's 'maritime' context brings out that the Indian Ocean Region (IOR) is an important cog and a wheel in its MSR initiative. The MSR presents unique opportunities and challenges to India in its immediate and extended maritime periphery. A policy response to this mix would involve shades of cooperation and competition requiring delicate balancing between its political, economic and military security imperatives.

Chapter Four by Irene Chan, emphasizes the importance of Southeast Asia's role in determining the success of the MSR. Given the asymmetric relations between ASEAN and China, it is argued that it is unlikely for ASEAN to endorse the MSR. However, the author emphasizes that it is important to understand the position of individual Southeast Asian states, especially the perspectives from Thailand, Vietnam, Malaysia, Singapore and Indonesia. China is both a regional player as well as an emerging global maritime power and, how well China can persuade its partners to focus on collective maritime interests and concerns, and more importantly, meeting of the various maritime security challenges ahead without being embroiled in existing regional political and strategic rivalry will greatly affect regional stability and security.

Divyank in Chapter Five proposes that China's 21st Century MSR could pave new trade routes and expand its economic linkages with Asia, Africa, and Europe. South Asian entrepots would be important nodes in realizing the potential of this strategy. However, the full viability of the MSR would be determined not only by the historically established Indian Ocean shipping lanes but also by the subcontinent's politico-economic context. This chapter examines the significance of South Asia for China's economic expansion and the region's diverse responses to the MSR proposal. This initiative could also serve to subsume the paradigm of Beijing Consensus by expanding China's reach to liberal market economies and refashioning its image of a mentor-patron of weak and, in some cases, authoritarian states.

In Chapter Six, Anatara proposes that since its introduction, the scope of the MSR project has widened and several countries in South Asia, Asia Pacific and Europe have supported the initiative. There is now a new trend of emphasis on the African continent in the MSR narratives. China's 'Africa push' is an important development in the geopolitics of Indian Ocean Region (IOR), which can have far-reaching consequences. It contextualizes MSR's Africa tilt apropos the evolving dynamics of China-Africa relationship by addressing certain critical questions, such as - how will the blueprint for MSR in Africa possibly look like, and; what is Africa's response to MSR. The Chapter also determines the implications - both challenges and opportunities - for India given its shared history and special relation with Africa.

In Chapter Seven, Kwa draws on the historical images and metaphors of ancient sealanes linking China to its south and west. To understand what the modern MSR may entail, the author provides a review of the deep historical linkages, not just of trade but of people, ideas, culture, religion and technologies. The historical narratives are often reconstructed and this new initiative could be seen as a 'new reconstruction' of the connected histories of the region. However, the larger question of the new narrative resonating among the potential partners still remains to answered.

In Chapter Eight, Adwita Rai argues that the 21st century initiatives by India and China 'Project Mausam' and 'MSR' have brought matters maritime into limelight. Both concepts since their inception aim at reviving and acknowledging maritime past through cooperation and collaboration. Although both inherit claims from the past, there is far lesser attention paid to the significance of reshaping 'Maritime History'. The Chapter draws convergences and divergence between the MSR and Mausam projects.

Given that MSR is a relatively new concept, the discourse on this issue is still evolving. As the projects and plans linked to MSR become more concrete, the narratives are also expected to take new shapes and newer directions. While the aspects covered in this volume address the 'broader big picture', the different themes examined by the authors do bring out the fact that MSR is an important initiative from China with global ramifications. It is hoped that this book will help further invigorate the debate on this issue.

-    Vijay Sakhuja and Jane Chan

1 Geopolitics of China's 'Maritime Silk Road' Concept: An Indian Perspective

Gurpreet S Khurana

"Practice is the sole criterion of truth...It doesn't matter whether a cat is white or black, so long as it catches mice."
- Deng Xiaoping

In October 2013, while on a visit to Indonesia, the Chinese President proposed "greater connectivity with ASEAN countries... (and) develop maritime partnership... to build the 'Maritime Silk Road' of the 21st century", commonly called the 'Maritime Silk Road' or MSR.[1] The concept draws from China's Han Dynasty era (206 BC-220 AD) when key land and sea trading routes carried Chinese silk to Europe.

To the Chinese, two contrasting concepts of 'symbolism' and 'realism' go hand-in-hand. Symbolism emerges from any idea that does not necessarily mirror reality – it could be an abstract or fictitious one, or a historic case, which may or may not be relevant to present times. But it is noteworthy, that the Chinese draw upon the idea innovatively, and apply it with finesse through a pragmatic realpolitik approach to meet their clear-sighted national objectives. The 'Maritime Silk Road' (MSR) initiative of President Xi Jinping is an example that represents a master-stoke of Chinese diplomacy, which for future generations, may well be considered a historic example of Chinese statecraft since the era of Mao Zedong.

Since the MSR concept was announced, China has approached all countries, particularly those strategically located along the shipping lanes stretching across the Western Pacific and the Indian Ocean, seeking their partnership. Notably, a major portion of the MSR lies across the Indian Ocean and its contiguous seas. In February 2014, China formally invited India to join the MSR.[2]

China claims that MSR is driven purely by an economic agenda. It involves China's engagement with the countries located along the MSR to enhance sea trade connectivity with its MSR partners through development of their ports and related infrastructure and developing economic-industrial zones in their hinterlands.[3] Through this, China claims that it is offering assistance to its MSR partners to boost trade-linked industrial productivity. MSR aims not only to make sea-transportation more efficient, but also shifting of China's low-end manufacturing industries to the economic-industrial zones of the MSR partners. While this would help China to address its industrial overcapacity and rising production costs, the MSR partner countries would gain through development of trade and industrial infrastructure. It would also help China to gainfully invest its surplus money into the MSR projects. China has also established the US$ 40 billion dedicated 'Silk Road Fund' and the Asian Infrastructure Investment Bank (AIIB) with an expected initial capital of US$50 billion, which may also be used to support China's Silk Road initiatives.[4]

In more comprehensive terms, however, MSR aims not only to bail out China from the current economic 'doldrums', but also uses 'economics' as effective 'camouflage' to achieve its national objectives in the Indo-Pacific region[5] and beyond through favourable geo-politics. The term 'geopolitics' may be defined as the interplay among countries based on their relative power, which is conditioned by the spatial, temporal, political, economic, security and legal aspects of international relations.[6]

This chapter examines MSR in context of China's likely grand-strategic objectives in the Indo-Pacific region, to assess how the concept transcends the domain of (pure) 'economics' into the ('economics plus') realm of broader geo-politics. It concludes by appraising China's approach in this direction.

MSR: Geopolitical Objectives

Regional Influence

MSR helps China to propagate influence in the Indo-Pacific region (its 'periphery'), and possibly beyond it. For Beijing, such influence is an overarching strategic objective for various reasons ranging from China's civilizational existence and recognition as the 'Middle Kingdom', to the contemporary realities of its 'rise' as a challenger to the global predominance of the United States and 'displacing' its influence in the Indo-Pacific region. While China is presently seeking the status of a global power alongside the US in a bipolar world, its longer term objectives may be more ambitious - possibly akin to the 'Middle Kingdom of the 21st century'.

China realises that its aim of being the global 'unipole' is not easy. It would need to overcome numerous challenges ranging from 'territorial consolidation' to re-orientation of the global economic and security architecture. This makes China a non-*status quo* power, whose foremost imperative would be to garner geo-political support of the regional countries and a univocal stance at international and regional fora. This is necessary for Beijing to shape the global order in its favour, and fructify its maritime and territorial claims.

China's regional influence is also necessary for assured access to natural resources and raw-material to feed its high-end manufacturing industries. It is pertinent to note that Beijing strongly believes in the dictum of 'flag follows trade' and is well known for its 'mercantilist' approach to economic growth. Towards this end, China began engaging the African countries a decade before the MSR was conceived. In the African context, therefore, MSR may be merely a platform to reinforce China's larger geopolitical ends, rather than a medium to forge mutually-beneficial economic partnerships with the African countries, such as through outsourcing Chinese manufacturing and investments to develop their trade infrastructure.

China is also seeking to increase its defence exports in the region. Between 2010 and 2014, China overtook Germany, France and the United Kingdom to become the world's third largest arms exporter (exporting five per cent of global sales), but lags far behind Russia in the second place (exporting 27 per cent).[7] MSR could also be used to shift low-end Chinese defence industry to the huge regional markets, thereby facilitating arms exports to the regional countries. This driver transcends 'economics', and goes into the domain of Beijing's 'national-strategic' objective to create a security dependence of the regional countries upon China. As MSR enables China's regional influence to facilitate its arms exports, Chinese-origin hardware being operated by IOR countries would accrue strong military-strategic dividends for China in terms of the sustenance of its naval forces in the Indian Ocean through overseas technical and ordnance support, virtually akin to 'overseas bases'.

Engaging Key Countries

Although China needs the support of all its prospective MSR partners, it is critically necessary for Beijing to bring a few key countries like Indonesia 'onboard'. Although it was first announced in Indonesia in September 2013, it is unlikely that the conception of MSR happened to coincide with President Xi Jinping's visit to Jakarta. It is more likely to have been deliberated well in advance, and 'timed' with the visit, considering that Indonesia bears a high potential to play a pivotal role in the geopolitics of the Indo-Pacific region. Furthermore, Indonesia's geographic location and disposition makes it cardinal for China's naval mobility in the Indo-Pacific region, across the Southeast Asia's maritime choke-points.

Sri Lanka is another key country, essentially in terms of its geo-strategic 'centrality' in the IOR vis-á-vis China's maritime energy 'lifelines', which President Xi Jinping may have referred to implicitly when he called Sri Lanka as the "hub" of MSR.[8] It may be recalled that eight years ago in March 2007, China signed an agreement with Sri Lanka to provide financial aid and technical support to develop Hambantota port located at the southern tip of Sri Lanka, only six nautical miles from the arterial shipping route of the Indian Ocean.[9] The choice of Colombo for the unprecedented visit of a Chinese submarine to the Indian Ocean in September 2014 is among the more recent indicators of the maritime-strategic salience of Sri Lanka. Notably, the submarine docked at the Colombo International Container Terminal, which has been constructed through financial assistance provided by China.[10]

India is another key prospective MSR partner. While New Delhi's participation may not be critical for the success of MSR's 'economic' agenda, its reticence would be a cause for grave concern for Beijing, particularly when seen in the light of India's increasing strategic convergence with the United States. In March 2014, the Chinese Ambassador to New Delhi proposed to merge MSR with the India's projects 'Mausam'[11] and 'Spice Route'.[12] The two Indian projects also have historical underpinnings, and widely seen as an Indian 'response' to the MSR.[13] Notably, the same month, the Indian Prime Minister visited the three Indian Ocean island countries (Seychelles, Mauritius and Sri Lanka), which was reported in the Chinese state-run daily *Global Times* as "a move to boost India's maritime influence". *Global Times* added that,

"...there is no easy way of persuading a rising power in China's neighbourhood to recognise that its mega project (MSR) is not seeking for influence or striving for hegemony... the recent remark that 'the One Belt and One Road initiatives can also be linked with India's Spice Route and Mausam projects,' by Chinese Ambassador to India Le Yucheng might provide a blueprint for cooperation that could create tangible benefits for both sides and help India to set suspicions aside."[14]

Whether the Chinese proposal carries any 'substantive' dividend for India may be debatable, but it is clearly an effort by Beijing to sway New Delhi through symbolism. Like the Chinese, will India combine symbolism with pragmatism? What would New Delhi do to resolve its 'MSR Dilemma'?

Pakistan is another key country for MSR, notwithstanding the fact that no ancient silk route touched any Pakistani port. For many years, the China-Pakistan Economic Corridor (CPEC) project has been central to China's strategy to gain access to the Indian Ocean for its underdeveloped west, and enhance its influence in the IOR. However, Pakistan's role in MSR seems to have been underplayed by China, possibly to cater for India's sensitivities.

Softening' China's 'Maritime Rise'

Since the turn of the new millennium, the Chinese leadership have emphasized on mobilizing nationalist feelings through the revival of China's 'maritime glory'. The glorification of voyages undertaken by the 15th century Chinese Admiral Cheng He is case in point.[15] Concurrently, Chinese naval power grew rapidly in both qualitative and quantitative terms. Such enhanced 'capacity' also increased China's 'self-confidence' to adopt an assertive politico-military posture towards its maritime-territorial claims in the Western Pacific.

Through 'economics' of MSR, China may have sought to 'dilute' the regional focus on its 'hard' (military) power, and also offset the adverse effects of its politico-military assertiveness. Secondly, by leveraging the enhanced MSR-related economic stakes, China could control escalation of conflict in such scenarios, and compel these countries to acquiesce to Beijing's will.

MSR may be seen as a counter to the theory of 'String of Pearls', which was propounded by a United States' think-tank,[16] but has since gained significant traction in Indian academic discourse. Before MSR was launched, China laboured hard to convince the regional countries that its port projects in the Indo-Pacific region were commercial, not military-strategic ventures. In end July 2013 (two months before the launch of MSR), the China's state-run daily *Global Times* carried an article saying,

> "China is stringing up a chain of pearls in the Indian Ocean – this expression has made many headlines in Indian newspapers. India, if we are to believe the forecasts of alarmist scholars, is going to wear a heavy and suffocating string of pearls...it is not true that China's involvement in the Indian Ocean (through port projects) bears ulterior motives under ostensibly commercial cover....these ports... might resemble 'string of pearls' that encircles India, but a strategy named after this fact is imaginary."[17]

Driven solely by an economic agenda, the MSR may have been considered by Beijing as a way to make the regional countries realize the 'truth' in what the Chinese were 'always saying'. While MSR would serve to 'trash' the western 'String of Pearls', it would enhance China's options for using the maritime facilities in IOR of replenishment of naval forces engaged in peace-time missions (like counter-piracy) and also short-of-war contingencies (akin to the US concept of 'places, not bases').

Response to US 'Rebalance'

The MSR may be seen as a response to the 'rebalance' strategy initiated by the United States in 2011.[18] Viewed from China's perspective, the strategy seeks to contain China within East Asia. The containment operates at the geopolitical level, involving economic, diplomatic, and military-strategic elements. The economic element of 'rebalance' seeks to isolate China through creation of US-led 'exclusive' blocks such as the Trans-Pacific Partnership (TPP).[19] The diplomatic element seeks to counter the increasing US politico-diplomatic engagement with its regional allies, 'partners' like India and other littoral countries. Potentially, the MSR could be used by Beijing as an effective counter to both the 'economic' and 'diplomatic' elements of the 'rebalance' strategy.

The MSR can also be seen as a military-strategic response to the 'rebalance' strategy of the United States. The strategy seeks a military-strategic containment of China through increasing military presence in the Western Pacific, and its *Joint (operational) Concept for Access and Maneuver in the Global Commons*' (JAM-GC). Through MSR, China could seek to project its naval power into the IOR, which could release the US strategic pressure in China's backyard. In February 2014, the PLA Navy task force crossed the Southeast Asian straits into the Indian Ocean to conduct unprecedented and unannounced exercises off northern Australia,[20] as if testing its concept of 'strategic distraction'.

Possibly some geopolitical aspects of MSR conceived above may not have been conceived by Beijing when MSR was launched. Nonetheless, the Chinese leadership is likely to capitalise on these opportunities from a realpolitik perspective.

'Wither' MSR

Soon after the MSR initiative was first announced in October 2013, the Chinese government launched an 'aggressive' region-wide MSR campaign to elicit support of the prospective partners. Likely to be a result of a top-down directive, the campaign involves all echelons of Chinese policy establishment ranging from the apex leadership to Chinese think-tanks organisations. It includes various activities ranging from inviting foreign officials and academia to MSR conferences in China; and to the out-bound visits at all levels ranging from the President to young scholars. During events conducted in China, in accordance with 'higher directives', the visiting delegates are accorded 'top-notch' hospitality, and all expenditure on this count is reimbursed by the Chinese government.

Beijing is likely supplement to the MSR initiative with other measures. An article by PLA's Major General Ji Mingkui of the Chinese National Defense University (NDU) recommends that for reinforcing MSR and overcoming the geopolitical risks and historical or cultural issues that might run counter to the concept, China "should mobilize the forces of overseas Chinese in countries along the route and encourage them" to use their "social resources to promote official and personal multi-level international cooperation."[21] The unprecedentedly quick reaction by the PLA Navy to evacuate Chinese citizens (along with foreign nationals) from Yemen in March-April 2015 may be seen in this context.[22]

The positive outcome of Beijing's MSR campaign is clearly discernible. For most developing countries of the Indo-Pacific region, the economic dividends of MSR are irresistible. Hopeful that China would replicate Japan's Flying Geese Paradigm (FGP) of the 1960s, these countries cannot afford to miss this 'opportunity'. With Japan as the 'lead goose', FGP was an economic model for division of labour in East Asia based on optimisation of comparative advantage, which resulted in the development of South Korea, Taiwan, Singapore, Hong Kong and other the participating economies (in the 'wild geese flying pattern'). [23]

Individually, countries are driven by their own geopolitical imperatives to support MSR. The geo-strategically disadvantaged Bangladesh, for example, seeks to 'connect' with China to avoid being 'boxed in' by the India. During the meeting between President Xi Jinping and Prime Minister Sheikh Hasina in June 2014, the two discussed both the BCIM Corridor Project and the MSR.[24] While MSR is a maritime 'extension' of the BCIM Project meant to foster economic connectivity, both bear a geopolitical rationale for Dhaka.

Among others, three key regional countries are likely to become China's MSR partners. On the eve of the visit of Indonesia's President Joko Widodo to China in end-March 2015, he indicated his desire to seek details of MSR so that he could endorse it.[25] Sri Lanka is likely to follow suit; notably, in his December 2014 pre-election manifesto, Sri Lanka's President Sirisena had expressed his intent to reconsider the US$1.4 billion Chinese-funded project to develop Colombo port. However, later events led to a "careful assessment" of the issue, following which, the Sri Lankan government indicated that it is likely to go ahead with the project.[26] In April 2015, a Chinese company was given a 40 year contract for operating Gwadar port.[27] A few days later, the Chinese President announced an investment of a mammoth US$ 46 billion for the China-Pakistan Economic Corridor (CPEC) project.[28] Notably, the same month, the Pakistani Prime Minister approved a deal to buy eight Chinese-built submarines.[29] These developments led the Indian Navy chief to remark that "We have our eyes firmly set on waters of interest around us. The navy is a multi-dimensional combat force and we are looking at all aspects related to sea control and sea denial amid the unfolding developments in the region".[30] Possibly, India remains the only country in the Indo-Pacific region that has not yet decided to join the MSR.

The MSR also capitalizes on the geopolitical outlook of the smaller regional countries – particularly those in Southeast Asia – who are prone to 'hedging'-cum-'bandwagoning'. Although these countries seek to 'hedge' against China, they will 'bandwagon' for a collective approach, even if it serves China's grand-strategic objectives. However, it remains to be seen whether the MSR 'bandwagon' would be able to 'displace' the influence of the United States among these countries.

Conclusion

The MSR is an element of China's broader 'March West' strategy that Beijing has adopted against what it perceives as geopolitical and strategic challenges imposed upon it by the United States and its allies in the Indo-Pacific region. However, as China 'marches west', it is likely to encounter India with its invigourated 'Act East' policy, which would have a significant import for the region; and in particular, for its relations with India that are characterised by an adversarial potential.

Given that the MSR bears facets and implications beyond 'pure economics', the Indian policymakers are understandably circumspect about the initiative. Besides, from the broader perspective, the MSR has emerged as an element of the intensifying geopolitical tussle between China and the United States. There is no reason for the 'Indian elephant' to allow itself to be trampled in the contest.

Notes and References

1   "Speech by Chinese President Xi Jinping to Indonesian Parliament", *ASEAN-China Centre*, 03 October 2013, http://www.asean-china-center.org/english/2013-10/03/c_133062675.htm (accessed 16 September 2014).

2   "China invites India to join its Maritime Silk Road initiative", *Economic Times*, 14 February 2014, http://articles.economictimes.indiatimes.com/2014-02-14/news/47337341_1_msr-special-representative-yang-jiechi-border-talks (accessed 15 November 2014).

3   "China accelerates planning to re-connect Maritime Silk Road", *Xinhua*, 16 April 2014, at http://www.globaltimes.cn/content/854988.shtml (accessed 16 December 2014).

4   "China pledges $40bn for Silk Road plan ahead of APEC summit", *Times of India*, 09 November 2014, at http://timesofindia.indiatimes.com/world/china/China-pledges-40bn-for-Silk-Road-plan-ahead-of-APEC-summit/articleshow/45085179.cms and "China invests in maritime silk road to fund port expansion", India Gazette, November 16, 2014, at http://www.indiagazette.com/index.php/sid/227672099 (both accessed 16 December 2014).

5   Refers to the region stretching from the littorals of East Africa and West Asia, across the Indian Ocean and Western Pacific Ocean, to the littorals of Northeast Asia. The term was first used in 2007 by the author in Khurana, Gurpreet S. (2007) 'Security of Sea Lines: Prospects for India-Japan Cooperation', *Strategic Analysis*, 31:1, 139 – 153.

6   This connotation is closely related to the erstwhile concept of (military) *Balance of Power*, that continues to be in vogue in present times, albeit in a broader sense of both 'hard' and 'soft' (including economic) power.

7   The US in the first place, with 31 per cent share of global exports. 'China becomes the world's third largest arms exporter', *BBC News*, 16 March 2015, http://www.bbc.com/news/technology-31901493 (accessed 27 March 2015).

8   "China hopeful of Colombo Project as Sri Lanka backs Silk Road", *India Today*, 26 March 2015, http://indiatoday.intoday.in/story/president-maithripala-sirisena-president-xi-jinping-maritime-silk-road-initiative/1/425874.html (accessed 28 March 2015).

9   Gurpreet S. Khurana, "China's 'String of Pearls' in the Indian Ocean and its Security Implications", *Strategic Analysis*, IDSA, Vol 32 (1), 2008, pp.1-39

10 Rajat Pandit, "India suspicious as Chinese submarine docks in Sri Lanka", *Times of India*, 28 September 2014, http://timesofindia.indiatimes.com/

india/India-suspicious-as-Chinese-submarine-docks-in-Sri-Lanka/ articleshow/43672064.cms (accessed 29 March 2015).

11 The Project was launched on 20 June 2014 at UNESCO's 38th World Heritage Session at Doha, Qatar. "Project Mausam", Ministry of Culture (Government of India) website, at http://www.indiaculture.nic.in/project-mausam (accessed 28 March 2015).

12 A heritage project initiated by the south Indian provincial state of Kerela, and supported by UNESCO. It is based on the ancient 2000-year-old Spice Route that connected 31 countries. "Kerala Tourism inks pact with UNESCO to preserve Spice Route heritage", *Business Line*, 02 August, 2014, http://www. thehindubusinessline.com/industry-and-economy/travel/kerala-tourism-inks-pact-with-unesco-to-preserve-spice-route-heritage/article6275259.ece (accessed 29 March 2015).

13 "China seeks India's 'Spice Route' link with its 'Silk Road'", *Times of India* (New Delhi), 06 March 2015, p.13.

14 "Cooperation best route for Beijing and Delhi over maritime objectives", *Global Times*, 26 March 2015, at http://www.globaltimes.cn/content/914139. shtml (accessed 29 March 2015).

15 The Beijing Olympic Games began on 08 August 2008, with a dramatic opening ceremony featuring the evocation of Admiral Zheng He.

16 The phrase 'String of Pearls' was first used in a 2005 report by Booz–Allen–Hamilton, 'Energy Futures in Asia' prepared for US Defense Secretary. '*String of Pearls* Military Plan to Protect China's Oil: US Report', *Space War*, 18 January, 2005, http://www.spacewar.com/2005/050118111727.edxbwxn8. html, (accessed 22 October 2007).

17 Hu Zhiyong, "India wears unreal <String of Pearls>", *Global Times*, 28 July, 2013, at http://www.globaltimes.cn/content/799641.shtml, (accessed 29 March 2015).

18 Opening Remarks by President Obama at APEC, Session One, *The White House*, Office of the Press Secretary, 13 November 2011, http://www. whitehouse.gov/thepress-office/2011/11/13/openingremarks-president-obama-apec-session-one.

19 "Economic Dimension of US 'Rebalance': A 'Back Door' to China's Containment?", *NMF Issue Brief*, National Maritime Foundation (NMF) New Delhi, 29 May 2014, http://www.maritimeindia.org/CommentryView. aspx?NMFCID=164, (accessed 28 March 2015).

20 Michael Brissenden, "RAAF Monitored Chinese Military Exercise in Waters between Christmas Island and Indonesia', *ABC Net News*, 13 February 2014,

http://www.abc.net.au/news/2014-02-13/china-flexed-military-muscle-north-of-australia/5257686, (accessed 28 March 2015).

21 China.org, 01 December 2014, at http://paper.people.com.cn/dnis/index.jsp cited in Nathan Beauchamp-Mustafaga, "Dispatch from Beijing: PLA Writings on the New Silk Road", *China Brief* (The Jamestown Foundation), Vol 15: 4, 20 February 2015, p.2.

22 Kevin Wang, "Yemen Evacuation a Strategic Step Forward for China", *The Diplomat*, 10 April 2015, http://thediplomat.com/2015/04/yemen-evacuation-a-strategic-step-forward-for-china/ (accessed 02 May 2015).

23 'The Flying Factory', *The Economist*, 15 November 2014, http://www.economist.com/news/special-report/21631799-asia-has-built-web-economic-interdependence-which-china-would-be-ill-advised For details, see Shigehisa Kasahara, 'The Asian Developmental State and the Flying Geese Paradigm', *UNCTAD* Discussion Paper No. 213, November 2013, at http://unctad.org/en/PublicationsLibrary/osgdp20133_en.pdf, (both accessed 08 April 2015).

24 'China and Bangladesh pledge to build 'Maritime Silk Road', *DVB News*, 11 June 2014, at http://www.dvb.no/dvb-video/china-and-bangladesh-pledge-to-build-maritime-silk-road-burma-myanmar/41423 (accessed 02 April 2015).

25 "Indonesia to throw open doors to Chinese investment; seeks details on maritime Silk road", *South China Morning Post*, 25 March 2015, http://www.scmp.com/print/news/asia/article/1746628/widodo-aims-use-china-visit-boost-ties-and-seek-details-maritime-silk-road, (accessed 08 April 2015).

26 "India's Approach to China's Maritime Silk Road: An Alternative View", *NMF Issue Brief*, National Maritime Foundation (NMF) New Delhi, 17 February 2015, http://www.maritimeindia.org/CommentryView.aspx?NMFCID=8390, (accessed 08 April 2015).

27 Saibal Dasgupta, "China gets 40-year management rights on Pak's Gwadar port, and access to Arabian Sea", *Times of India*, 14 April 2015, http://timesofindia.indiatimes.com/world/china/China-gets-40-year-management-rights-on-Paks-Gwadar-port-and-access-to-Arabian-Sea/articleshow/46923252.cms (accessed 20 April 2015).

28 "China's Xi Jinping agrees $46bn superhighway to Pakistan", *BBC News*, 20 April 2015, http://www.bbc.com/news/world-asia-32377088 (accessed 27 April 2015).

29 "Pakistan PM approves deal to buy eight Chinese submarines: official", *Reuters*, 02 April 2015, http://www.reuters.com/article/2015/04/02/us-china-pakistan-idUSKBN0MT05M20150402, (accessed 26 April 2015).

30   Rahul Singh, "India keeping a close eye on China-Pak military cooperation: Navy chief", *Hindustan Times*, 20 April 2015, at http://www.hindustantimes. com/india-news/we-re-closely-tracking-developments-in-chinese-navy- and-ready-for-any-eventuality-admiral-dhowan/article1-1339001.aspx, (accessed 20 April 2015).

2 | China's "One Belt, One Road" Initiative: The Convergence of Strategic Interests and Domestic Imperatives

Mingjiang Li

Chinese president Xi Jinping put forth the Silk Road Economic Belt and the 21st Century Maritime Silk Road (MSR) proposals, also known as the "One Belt, One Road" Initiative (BRI), during his visits to Kazakhstan and Indonesia in September and October 2013 respectively.

The BRI has become a priority in China's foreign and domestic policies. Reports and analyses on the topic have inundated the Chinese media. The initiative has also become the most popular term in the community of International Relations (IR) scholars in China. Numerous Chinese IR scholars and analysts in many other fields, including international economics and trade, have begun research on the BRI. It is perhaps no exaggeration to say that the scale and intensity of Chinese research on this subject are unprecedented. In fact, the zeal of Chinese researchers in jumping on board to study this policy proposal has led some Chinese colleagues joke that there exists a "Belt-and-Road Party" in China. This clearly reflects the importance that the Chinese political leadership attaches to this new initiative.

Although the initiative is much-discussed at almost every major international affairs forum or conference in China, the outside world either does not seem too excited over it or perhaps has overlooked its significance. This chapter attempts to explain the rationale behind the Chinese proposal and the challenges that China may face in the implementation of the initiative. The paper argues that this initiative represents the convergence of China's international strategic interests and domestic imperatives. Beijing is inclined to carry out this blueprint regardless of the obstacles it may face.

China's Grand Strategy

There is no doubt that the BRI is a grand Chinese strategy. This grand strategy emerged because of a few reasons. First, it reflected the end of China's debate whether China should continue to adhere to the "low profile" international strategy. The late Chinese leader Deng Xiaoping proposed the "low profile" strategy for China's foreign policy in the early 1990s soon after the Tiananmen Incident when China was politically isolated and facing difficulties dealing with the United States and other Western powers. For many years, that strategy was, to a large extent, observed by the Jiang Zemin and Hu Jintao administrations on the grounds that confronting the West and assuming too many international responsibilities would not benefit China's development. However, starting in the mid-2000s, many Chinese strategists began to challenge this strategic view and advocated gradually abandoning the "low profile" strategy. And by the late 2000s, there was almost consensus in China that the "low profile" strategy needed to be at least significantly amended: China needed to adopt a more proactive international strategy to help shape a new international and regional order. The BRI has to be understood in this context of strategic debate in China.

China's interest in adopting a more proactive international posture and increasing its influence in the world was significantly augmented in the wake of the global financial crisis in the late 2000s. When much of the rest of the world, especially the developed Western world, was hit hard by the financial crisis, the Chinese economy experienced rapid growth. As a result, many Chinese elites felt more confident about China's development model and China's growing power. Beijing had high expectations about the upcoming reforms of the global financial system. These reforms were expected to reflect the changing balance of power and give China more decision-making authority in some of the major international institutions such as the World Bank and the International Monetary Fund. The promised reform package of allocating a bigger role for China did not materialize. Beijing was clearly very frustrated when the US Congress failed to approve the proposed reforms of these institutions. The failure of these reforms, to a large extent, propelled China to seek alternative options. This explains China's zealous support for the development bank of the BRICS grouping. It is perhaps a primary reason for Beijing's push for the Asian Infrastructure Investment Bank (AIIB).

Second, the BRI is built on China's successful diplomacy in the past two decades. China's international profile has been significantly upgraded and its influence in many parts of the world has been noticeably increased. This success, to a very large extent, is attributable to China's economic engagements with other countries. Beijing's growing economic clout in Africa has been well documented. In East Asia, many analysts believe that China significantly changed the regional order by carving out a leading role in regional trade and economics. It has been frequently highlighted that China has become the biggest trading partner for most countries in the region. Many pundits even believe that we now have a dual regional structure in East Asia: the United States plays the leading role in the strategic and security arena while China plays the leading role in regional trade and economics.

Given the size of China's economy and market, economic relations between many regional states and China are essentially asymmetric and work in China's favor. These asymmetric economic ties benefited China's regional security. For example, it is now increasingly more and more difficult for the Association of Southeast Asian Nations (ASEAN) to stand up against China in the South China Sea disputes despite strong lobbying from some ASEAN member states such as Vietnam and the Philippines. It is also now far more challenging for many regional states to strategically realign with Washington against China. Asymmetric economic ties brought Beijing commercial benefits, as well as strategic and security advantages. Thus, it is no surprise that China began to contemplate a new grand strategy in Asia in the late 2000s, one or two years before the United States started talking about a strategic rebalance to the Asia Pacific. Beijing came up with the BRI strategy in this context, hoping to further take advantage of its growing economic power to expand Chinese influence in Asia and beyond.

Third, the BRI is China's response to the growing strategic rivalry between China and other major players, especially the United States. In private conversations, many Chinese colleagues suggested that China's attempt to downplay the strategic dimensions of the initiative is indeed partly a response to the strategic realignments happening in China's neighborhood in the past few years, particularly the US strategic rebalance to Asia. Despite Washington's constant clarification that the United States has no intention to contain China, many analysts in China insist that the US strategic rebalance is targeted at China. Many Chinese analysts take issue with America's growing military presence and expanding security ties with many countries in China's neighborhood. While it is widely believed that Beijing has been too assertive in handling the East and South China Seas disputes, the mainstream view among Chinese officials and observers is that all the tensions and disputes in the past few years were caused by US collaboration with China's neighboring states. Concerned about many regional states' active support for US strategic rebalance, Beijing decided to build closer security ties with Washington. In the light of these changing strategic realignments, some Chinese strategists proposed a "Look West" strategy. They argued that instead of confronting the United States head-on in the Asia Pacific, China could expand its influence westward by diverting part of its attention and resources to further engage with countries in China's western flank. Leaders in Beijing realized that the BRI may help ease some regional countries' growing apprehension of China and at the same time, enable China to compete with the United States in Asia. While the security tensions and disputes from 2009 to 2012 hindered the Chinese search for such a grand strategy, they also incentivized the Chinese decision makers to develop big policy initiatives to mitigate the perceived growing negativity in China's neighborhood.

Fourth, the major factor behind China's BRI has to do with the personality and ambition of China's new leader Xi Jinping. Compared to his predecessors, Xi is a far more nationalist and ambitious leader. Coming from a revolutionary family background, Xi is on a mission to consolidate the political rule of the Chinese Communist Party in China and significantly upgrade China's status in the world.

A New Round of Opening Up Drive

Chinese officials claim that the BRI is also part of the new round of China opening up. There is certainly a lot of truth in this claim. First, China is facing challenges of overproduction and overcapacity, particularly in the steel and construction materials sectors. China's manufacturing overcapacity is a result of China's model of economic growth in the past decades. Unlike many other countries, the Chinese government played an important role in boosting China's economic growth. Heavy investment in infrastructure and in the manufacturing sector has been a notable feature in China's success story. But there are limitations to the extent a government can and need to invest in the economy. By the late 2000s, it was already quite obvious that the manufacturing and construction sectors were facing serious overcapacity problems. China's policy in dealing with the financial crisis of 2008–2009 further worsened the overproduction issue. The central government decided to pump RMB 4 trillion into the economy to prevent a major economic slowdown. The local governments across China invested a much larger sum in the economy. Many more projects to improve infrastructure and manufacturing facilities were carried out. A few years later, such excessive investment resulted in an overheated Chinese economy. When the Chinese decision makers realized that China's manufacturing overproduction could not be resolved by domestic consumption, they decided to create more overseas demands by pursuing the BRI as a remedy for China's domestic economic problems.

Second, there is now a growing need for China to invest more and more in foreign countries. As labor costs rise, China will move its labor-intensive and low value-added manufacturing facilities to other countries. Over the decades, the low-end manufacturing facilities have created huge environmental problems for China. In these contexts, the Chinese government has, for many years, planned to significantly upgrade China's manufacturing sector as part of its overall economic restructuring strategy. The BRI could help China implement these economic policies.

Third, for China's interior and western provinces that have lagged far behind in the past decades of the opening-up drive, the initiative is likely to stimulate economic growth. Fourth, China has become a net capital exporter so the initiative will provide opportunities for an increasing number of Chinese investors on the lookout for investment opportunities overseas.

Since the reform and opening up in the late 1970s, China has labored to introduce foreign direct investment. It has also acquired advanced technologies and upgraded its management expertise with the help of other developed countries. China has been largely at the receiving end in terms of international rules, norms, and practices. Having experienced over three decades of rapid economic growth, China appears to be at the initiating end in many areas. The "going out" stage has just started for China. In this sense, it is perhaps fair to say that the BRI is indeed part of China's new round of opening up.

The Emerging Policy Substance

A few facts would demonstrate how seriously China regards the initiative. The belt and road proposal was included in the Resolution of the Third Plenum of the 18th Central Committee of the Chinese Communist Party, a historical document on the new leadership's push for a new round of comprehensive reforms in China. The Eighth meeting of the Central Leadership Group on Financial and Economic Affairs, chaired by Xi, specifically deliberated on the BRI in November 2014. At the annual central conference on economic affairs in December 2014, the initiative was highlighted as one of the priorities for China in 2015. In March 2015, the Chinese foreign minister Wang Yi announced that working on the BRI would be the central task in China's diplomacy and foreign affairs for the year. In the history of the People's Republic of China's foreign relations, there has never been another case that one particular policy issue was identified as the central task.

China has taken follow-up actions as well. It has launched the AIIB and set up a USD 40 billion Silk Road Fund. The BRI was showcased to many foreign leaders during the Beijing APEC meetings. From all accounts, the BRI has become China's national strategy. Very likely, the initiative will be regarded by Xi as a major foreign policy legacy at the end of his tenure.

The Chinese National Development and Reform Commission (NDRC), with support from relevant agencies, has developed and publicized a vision and action document for the BRI. According to Chinese documents, the "One Belt" runs from China to Central Asia, West Asia, Russia/Eastern Europe and Western Europe. The "One Road" connects China's coastal provinces to Southeast Asia, South Asia, the Middle East, North/East Africa, and Europe. The Maritime Silk Road will also connect Chinese ports to the South Pacific countries. Chinese pundits noted that as many as 65 countries would be included in the initiative. According to the vision and action document, any country or international organization in the world that would be interested in participating in the initiative could be counted as a participant.

This document suggests that the initiative will include five areas of connectivity: policy, facilities (including infrastructure), trade, finance, and people-to-people exchanges. More specifically, the implementation of the initiative would involve trade and investment facilitation measures;

infrastructure development (railways, highways, airports, ports, telecommunications, energy pipelines, and logistics hubs); industrial and sub-regional economic cooperation (primarily overseas industrial parks and economic corridors); financial cooperation and the promotion of people-to-people exchanges. The document includes many details on more important projects and the prioritization of areas of cooperation. For instance, when it comes to people-to-people exchanges, it is stated in the document that the Chinese government is prepared to provide as many as 10,000 scholarships for students along the "Belt and Road" lines.

The vision and action document stipulates that the implementation of the BRI follows the principles of close consultation, joint effort, and benefit-sharing. All participating countries will be expected to work closely to ensure proper coordination of their respective national development strategies. The ultimate goal of the initiative is to achieve broader, higher-level, and deeper regional cooperation. It is emphasized in the document that the implementation will abide by market mechanisms.

Challenges for the BRI

Some pundits pointed out that the BRI is largely *old wine in a new bottle*. There is much truth to this assertion. The initiative is not an entirely new plan for regional or sub-regional cooperation. China and many other regional countries worked on almost all the areas covered by the BRI. Such projects include the Greater Mekong River Sub-regional Cooperation (the GMS), Myanmar-China oil and gas pipelines, the various cross-border economic zones between China and a few neighboring countries, the second Eurasia Land Bridge, and the various existing Free Trade Agreements. What is different in the BRI is the fact that now we have a *more integrated* approach to all these cooperation schemes. For instance, the initiative emphasizes the integration and smooth connection of land, maritime, and air transport routes. If successful, this will significantly improve the efficiency of transportation and logistical services across the Eurasian continent. In this sense, there is also some *new wine* in the BRI policy package.

There is certainly a lot of old wine in the new BRI bottle. But the fact that the *bottle is much bigger* now is of equal relevance. Moreover, there is fairly more capable manager of the brewery—China. Beijing appears to have the political will, the experience, and the financial resources to play a leading role in pushing for and carrying out many projects that are outlined in the vision and action document. However, the initiative is not a well-thought-out scheme. The Chinese policy makers acknowledge that no comprehensive study was conducted before Xi proposed the BRI. It was only after Xi announced the proposal that the Chinese authorities and research institutes began to seriously study this initiative and prepare for the vision and action outline. Because of this, there has been no concrete implementation plan for the BRI. Even today, the Chinese officials acknowledge that they are still in search of modes of cooperation with other countries.

The BRI is not a plan without debate and controversy in China. In fact, in the past year or so, many Chinese analysts have been openly critical of the initiative, arguing that the plan is too ambitious, and fraught with political and economic risks. Some analysts fear that the decision makers may be too eager to implement the plan without paying enough attention to those risks.

Although most countries concerned have expressed their support, the initiative has also met with indifference and opposition from some countries. In Southeast Asia, Vietnam presented an ambivalent position on the MSR plan; similarly, the Philippines and Myanmar expressed their reservations about carrying out major projects with China. India demonstrated significant opposition to the MSR. Russia has officially accepted the Silk Road Economic Belt idea; in reality, it remains uncommitted to cooperating with China to implement the plan in Central Asia. Reluctance on the part of the United States and Japan may serve as further obstacles for the successful implementation of the BRI as well. Given the fierce competition between the Chinese and Japanese high-speed railway companies in Indonesia, it is evident that the implementation of the initiative could be a fairly complicated process.

Ideally, the BRI should be carried out in a multilateral manner. Beijing does hope to be able to receive support from various multilateral institutions such as ASEAN, the Shanghai Cooperation Organization (SCO), Asia-Europe Meeting (ASEM), etc. But in reality, it will be a significant challenge for China to succeed in getting all these institutions to endorse the initiative. ASEAN as a grouping, for instance, has not openly supported the MSR proposal, partly due to its consensus principle. Very likely, the initiative could only be implemented *bilaterally* between

China and those countries that are eyeing the economic benefits from cooperation with China. But the bilateral approach will have a significant negative impact on the proposed objective of seamless connectivity in facilities, trade policies, information sharing, and industrial cooperation.

Conclusion

The BRI appears to be an unprecedented proposal made by China in the history of contemporary Chinese foreign relations. It reflects the convergence of China's international strategic interests and domestic economic imperatives. Clearly, Beijing is seriously committed to the strategy. Beijing has worked hard in lobbying various countries to support and participate in the BRI. The Chinese media and various institutions have extensively explained the benefits that other countries may gain from the plan. The Chinese government has sponsored many forums in China and in other countries to promote the BRI idea.

Partly because of a lack of sufficient information about the BRI, the responses from many countries are still not very clear. Many countries will also continue to raise various political and national security concerns. Ultimately, they will balance the economic benefits of the BRI with their strategic and national security concerns. China seems to be anxious to start the initiative as soon as possible. Chinese reports indicate that progress has been made in Russia, Kazakhstan and Pakistan. More projects may be undergoing negotiations. Given China's determination and capabilities, it is very likely that the BRI will go ahead between China and those willing countries in the near future.

Security Dimension of China's 21st Century Maritime Silk Road –Indian Ocean Context

Raghavendra Mishra

China's Ambassador to India espoused a synergy between the Maritime Silk Road (MSR) and India's Project Mausam as these are grounded in similar, if not congruent, foundational precepts. The two principal commonalities between these initiatives are of historical recall and an attempt to break away from the existing 'clichéd discourse' on Asian maritime character. The larger narrative for China's Silk Road initiative has developed and expanded using two paths, one each addressing the terrestrial and oceanic domains. The Chinese President, Xi Jinping, mooted the 21st Century MSR concept during his address to the Indonesian Parliament in October 2013, particularly for strengthening China-ASEAN economic relationship.[1] Less than a month earlier, he laid out the broad contours of the land-centric Silk Road Economic Belt (SREB) in his September 2013 address at the Nazarbayev University, Kazakhstan.[2] Both initiatives are linked to Xi Jinping's call for the "great renewal of Chinese nation", dubbed as the 'China Dream' that draws upon its glorious civilizational history and status of a global great power.[3]

China has publicly emphasized the economic centrality, infrastructure development, regional connectivity, inclusiveness and people-to-people connect as the bedrock of Silk Road initiatives. However, the larger implications of the Silk Road initiatives cannot be overlooked as Silk Road initiatives are a strategic outreach to dispel the negative connotations arising out of its recent assertiveness on maritime/territorial disputes. The issue now also becomes important in the light of empirical-historical evidence about the behaviour of rising 'great powers'. More often than not, such nations have attempted to match their military potential to the geography of their global interests.

The Chinese official media, *Xinhua*, mentions discrete geographies for the SREB (China's coastal area through Central Asia, the Middle East and on to Europe) and MSR (China's south to Southeast Asia).[4] However, a different picture emerges by analysing the Chinese leadership discussions with countries across an extended Eurasian geo-spatial framework where it has encouraged them to join the MSR initiative. The list of such countries *inter alia* includes a number of Indian Ocean littorals like Bangladesh, India, Kuwait, Maldives, Myanmar, Oman, Pakistan, and Sri Lanka. In recent times with growing frequency, writings from China suggest that Africa should also be made part of the MSR for a providing a more holistic supra-regional contextualization.[5]

While the discourse among the majority of analytical community has addressed the SREB and MSR as distinct and separate entities, the correspondence in the spread of their geographies indicate that the idea of 'One Belt – One Road' (OBOR)' concept is a network. This is also evident from the 28 March 2015 unveiling of broad policy framework and composite principles for the Belt and Road initiative at Hainan during the Boao Forum for Asia (BFA).[6] The main aim is improved economic flows through efficient resource allocation for deeper market integration. This is to be achieved by enhancing connectivity of the Asian, European and African continents and their adjacent seas through an inclusive architecture (Figure 1).

This web of connectivity has various shades of maritimity, continentality and a mixed character (land-sea or the littoral interface) in its extent from China to the Western Europe.[7] This chapter seeks to analyse the security imperatives of the MSR through an Indian Ocean context. The theoretical approach employed is to undertake a systemic (global) to regional approach including a bilateral perspective of India-China interactions. Some factors taken into account while developing the analysis are: (a) amorphous international architecture; (b) increasingly globalised economy marked by uncertain trends; (c) growing relevance of oceans as critical spaces for traditional and rising powers in geopolitical and geo-economic terms; and, (d) the enhanced strategic relevance of maritime domain for China .

Figure 1. Geography of Silk Road Initiatives

Source: Xinhua, *China unveils action plan on Belt and Road Initiative*, 28 March 2015

Current and Future Geo-strategic Relevance of Oceans

Historically, Oceans are considered as the world's oldest commons covering roughly 70 percent of Earth's surface and considering their international character served as trans-continental arteries for global economy, trade, international commerce and ideational exchanges such as the spread of religion, socio-cultural norms, and literary thought. In a complimentary sense, the receding jurisdictional or 'control' regime at sea lends strong intimate linkages to international political dimensions of 'power' and 'influence' especially during times of flux and nebulosity, as is the case today.[8] This unbroken historical rhythm acquires relevance if one was to frame the strategic narratives of the important Indian Ocean stakeholders, such as:

  (a) *Australia* – Its emphasis is on the term 'Indo- Pacific' as a critical positive-cum-negative geography in its security strategy and other doctrinal publications.

  (b) *China* - 'March West' policy as a possible to counter US pivot strategy besides the MSR initiative.

(c) *India* – 'Act East' policy as a follow up of its Look East policy, and the recently announced Link West or Connect Central Asia initiative.

(d) *Indonesia* - President Jokowi's vision of 'Global Maritime Nexus' where Indonesia could be the fulcrum or the 'axis' for an interconnected the Pacific and Indian Ocean (PACINDO) domain.

(e) *Japan* – Its '*dual* hedge strategy' of reinforcing its security partnership with the US and, simultaneously seeking enhanced strategic engagements with South and South East Asia. Prime Minister Shinzo Abe's 2007 speech to the Indian Parliament titled "Confluence of the Two Seas" also merits recall.

(f) *Russia* – Its *recent* assertiveness in and around the proverbial Middle Sea (or the *Mediterranean*), especially in Syria and Ukraine. Further, the recent announcement about upgrading naval capabilities on its Pacific seaboard, i.e., 'Pivot to the East' can be seen as a significant policy shift.

(g) *United States* – Rebalance to Asia-Pacific coupled with more robust articulation about the strategic utility of seapower besides the coinage of a new geographic construct, 'Indo-Asia-Pacific' in its recently unveiled maritime strategy can be cited as some examples.

The important point to note from the above is that China is emphasizing an Indo-Atlantic construct through the Silk Road initiatives while the others have highlighted the enhanced relevance of the Indian and the Pacific Oceans. The second noteworthy issue is that the Indian Ocean finds common mention in all the strategic discourses, which indicates its growing importance as a critical maritime space. Given the embayed geography of the Indian Ocean, the littoral context - where air-sea-land domains intersect and affect each other through mutual interaction, would assume greater relevance while examining the strategic imperatives of the MSR project. This proposition is also supported by the mention of Bangladesh-China-India-Myanmar (BCIM) Economic Initiative and China-Pakistan Economic Corridor (CPEC) as vital 'tributaries' of the MSR.[9]

Theorising China's Maritime-cum-Naval Strategic Character

China's quest for greater maritime influence coupled with naval capability accretion, discussed in detail later in the chapter, could also be cast along some existing and some emerging theoretical curves. In a similar vein, the security dimension of MSR in relation to China can be developed along various thematic contours. Some of the salient concepts are :

(a) Taking historical recall as a point of departure, one description could be based on the mercantilism-cum-expeditionary approach, as practised by the behaviour of naval powers in the past, especially the former colonial powers.[10] Some Asian nations also practised a modified version of tributary system (formal inequality) in their episodic heydays of maritime eminence but their modern historiography has transmogrified these into more 'anodyne avatars'.[11] However, the utility of these theoretical axioms is somewhat restricted in present day globalised intermeshing.

(b) The second narrative could be built around the politico-diplomatic (policy)-economics-security circular cycle where each of these ·elements mutate and provide mutual reinforcements to larger strategic objectives through 'security-development nexus'.[12] In this regard, the 'naysayers' could argue, with some justification, on two counts; first being the 'tension-suppressing' effect of enhanced economic engagements on competitive-conflictual issues (trade–security nexus) as the mutual stakes become higher. The other disagreement could be on the exclusion of ideology-cum-informational aspects.[13] However, the opposition in both these cases are restrictive, archaic and built along binary lines and, thus relatively less relevant for application in the prevailing international climate. Further, the axiom that good economics translates into good politics and thereby more stability and security fails the historical empirical test. The important instances are the Anglo-German rivalries prior to the onset of the two world wars where these two countries were closely linked in economic sense but had contrarian outlooks as far as their 'strategic' aims were concerned.

(c) The next is the oft-quoted 'long cycle' framework where an 'enhanced external foreign policy orientation' of the rising powers drives the focus on to the 'oceans for strategic purposes' and their 'quest for dominant influence' on two of three perennially navigable water bodies, namely, the Pacific, Atlantic, and the Indian Oceans.[14] Another complementary approach in this regard could be the concept of 'using geography to trump strategic limitations' as espoused by the German Admiral Wolfgang Wegener in the interwar years.[15] In this context, the relevance of hyphenated constructs like Asia-Pacific and Indo-Pacific and others mentioned earlier, gain salience. A recent assessment of Chinese naval power states that its naval strategic approach is based on an 'offensive realist' model where Beijing is likely to seek absolute dominance and pre-eminence in the maritime realm.[16]

(d) The last, but not the least, is the quest by the great and rising powers for preferential strategic access to build mutualities and dependencies, such as, the 'String of Pearls' concept.[17] As part of this conceptual point of reference, other discourses could also be built along the continuums of 'affluence-arms-history-nationalism'.[18] A further tack could be to analyse Chinese strategic approach by analysing and the 'alignment of geopolitics-geography-geostrategy' by the great powers.[19]

The above theorems, in some measure or the other can be used to frame the current and future security imperatives of China in the Indian Ocean.

China's Maritimity and the Indian Ocean Context

A recent work suggests that in contemporary environment of enhanced economic meshing and globalised nature of strategic transactions between states, the factor of 'geo-economics' is the driver for the politics and the security policies of major powers.[20] In this case, it is argued that the classical geopolitical concepts of 'Heartland' proposed by Mackinder and that of 'Rimland' by Nicholas Spykman can be replaced by an emerging paradigm of seeking 'dominant access and influence' through a new geographical contextualisation of 'Nareland' (Natural Resource Lands). It is also argued that China is attempting to replace the traditional great powers like the US and Russia by positioning itself as a 'viable alternative strategic partner'. It is considered useful to examine the validity of this novel paradigm by applying it to the Chinese MSR concept, with particular reference to the IOR.

China's tack to the seas can be broadly equated to the geo-economics since sea borne trade remains the most economical means of transporting large volumes over long distances. As the world's leading exporting nation, second largest economy and trading nation by any yardstick of measurement and, as the largest shipbuilder, the oceans have become critical for its continued development.[21] This can be best farmed by examining the sectoral distribution of its economy and the part played by exports and imports in the post liberalisation period (Figure 2). In 1982 –when Deng Xiaoping's reforms were in the implementation phase, the industries contributed 44.8 percent to its GDP whereas the shares of agriculture and services sectors were 33.4 percent and 21.8 percent respectively. By 2013, a remarkable turnaround has taken place where the contribution of industry sector was 43.9 percent that of services sector had gone up to 46.1 percent of national GDP and the agriculture sector share had come down to 10 percent. This is reflective of a significant increase in the valued added productivity in the Chinese economy. Further, in 1982, the exports and imports of goods and services as a factor of GDP contributed 15.1 percent to the GDP, whereas, in 2013, this figure stood at 50.1 percent of national GDP, thus registering more than threefold growth over a 30-year period.

Figure 2. Sectoral distribution and contribution of Exports/Imports to Chinese Economy (percentage of GDP),

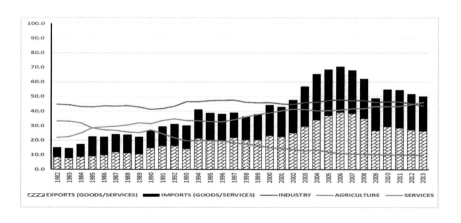

Source: World Bank Database, Authors Compilation

China's regional trade statistics during 2003-2013 indicate that Asia, Africa and, Oceania and Pacific Islands are the three regions where Beijing has an unfavourable trade balance (Appendix A). The Indian Ocean Region (IOR), comprising the littoral and the landlocked/Geographically Disadvantaged States (GDS) that are proximal to its coast, contribute nearly 20 percent of China's international trade in value terms (Appendix B). This trend of negative trade balance is more pronounced in the IOR, be it the share of the Asian or the African states. Saudi Arabia, Iran, Iraq, Kuwait, Oman, and South Africa are the principal contributing countries to this trend, thereby indicating the energy and mineral dependency of China in the IOR. The negative trade balance with Thailand can be attributed to the imports of automotive and telecom/IT industry sub-aggregates.

Beijing's dependence on Middle East oil imports of around 29 percent, as the share of its total consumption, is relatively less as compared to India (70 percent), Japan (76 percent) and Singapore (80 percent) (Figure 3). However, the oil imports sourced from the Middle East show a rising trend and, if the additional 15 percent share from the West African sources is also factored (as these traverse the Indian Ocean waters), the overall figure becomes a significant 45 percent of total national consumption.

China's quest for expanding geo-economic space for manoeuvre, seeking new avenues and opportunities in emerging markets and new geographies remains a key theme for current discourse. In this dialectic, China is projected in both negative and positive hues. The adverse narratives paint it as a nation bent on a commodities centric push for resource hoarding through unscrupulous means. The favourable analyses posit that China offers better and more competitive propositions as compared to the condition-linked regimes offered by the West and the rest.[22]

China's Naval Dynamics

Besides the dominant themes of economics and maritime commerce, China's naval modernisation in the 21st century has emerged as key topic for discussion among the analytical community. The refurbishment and commissioning of *Liaoning* aircraft carrier is one such example and reports suggest that more such platforms would join the ranks of the People's Liberation Army (Navy) (PLAN) by 2025.[23] A sustained and well

Figure 3. Middle East Oil Dependence (2009-13): Select Countries
(in Million Tonnes)

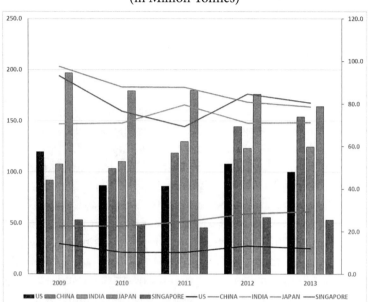

Source: Annual BP Statistical Reviews of World Energy, author's
Compilation

rounded, multi-dimensional accretion programme with a mix of offensive and defensive capabilities with longer reach and sustainability is apparent by the induction of modern platforms and systems since 2000. [24] Some examples are:

(a) Four Sovremenny class destroyers ex-import from Russia.

(b) Type 052 B/C/D (Luyang I/II/III) and Type 051C (Luzhou) class destroyers and Type 054A (Jiangkai II class) multi-purpose frigates.

(c) Type 056 (Jiangdao class) missile corvettes and Type 022 (Houbei class) missile craft.

(d) Type 903 (Fuchi) class replenishment ships, and; Type 071 (Yuzhao) and Type 072A (Yuting III) class amphibious assault ships.

(e) Type 094 (Jin) class SSBN (nuclear powered ballistic missile capable), Type 093 (Shang) class SSN (nuclear powered attack), and Type 039A (Yuan) class SSK (conventional diesel electric) submarines.

(f) Development of J-15 carrier borne strike and multirole Long-Range Maritime Reconnaissance version of H-6 aircraft.

(g) DF-21D Anti-Ship Ballistic Missile (ASBM).

(h) Conformal radars and multi-functional vertical launch systems on board the aircraft carrier, and Luyang III destroyers.

The Chinese naval modernisation programme is unique for a few reasons. While the availability of capital as the world's second largest military spending nation has helped, according to *IHS Janes Defence Budget* analysis, the PLA (N) continues to be the least funded among the conventional forces. However, consequent to the 2004 pronouncement of 'new historic missions', the importance of the navy has grown and its share of national budget is expected to increase from 18.6 percent in 2012 to 20.7 percent by 2020 [Figure 4(a)] . The report goes on to state that "In proportional terms the navy is expected to see the largest expansion of manpower and budgetary resources over the next decade and is expected to command an annual budget in the region of US $ 30 billion by 2016". Due to the proposed expansion plans the expenditure pattern on various sub-heads within the Navy is not likely to see a major shift, except for cutting down on miscellaneous expenses to improve operational effectiveness [Figure 4(b)].[25]

Figure 4(a): Inter-service Breakdown of Chinese Defence Budget (in percentage terms)	Figure 4(b): Sector wise Breakdown of PLA(N) Budget (in percentage terms)

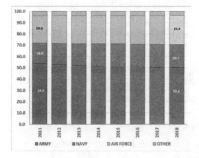 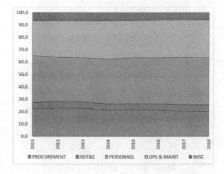

Source: IHS Janes, *Defence Budget - China*; 2014 copyrighted material, used with permission

One aspect that does not find adequate discussion is the Chinese 'defence economics' facet. For a nation with just US $ 302 million worth of military exports in 2000, China has emerged as the third largest supplier of defence equipment totalling US $ 2068 million in 2013. This represents almost seven-fold increase over a short period of 13 years and China has left behind some of the traditional military powerhouses like the UK, France, Netherlands and Israel [Figure 5(a)]. Asia and Africa are the prime locus of Chinese defence exports. During the period 1995-2013, Asia accounted for 79 percent of Chinese defence exports whereas Africa accounted for 18 percent (Figure 5(b)). Further, Pakistan, Bangladesh and Myanmar are the top three recipients accounting for roughly 68 percent of Chinese military exports during the five-year period of 2000-14. This fact was highlighted by this author and has been emphasised by Stockholm International Peace Research Institute (SIPRI) in its recent report on international arms transfer trends.[26]

Figure 5(a): Military Exports by Select Countries: 1995-2013 (in US $ million, constant 1990 terms)	Figure 5(b): Regional Distribution of Chinese Military Exports: 1995-2013 (in US $ million, constant 1990 terms)

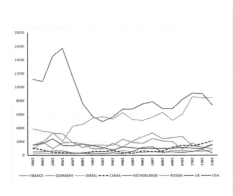 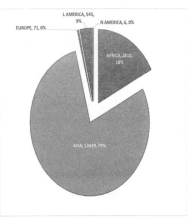

Source: SIPRI, Trend Indicator Value (TIV) Database, author's compilation

The noteworthy aspect is the deployment of Chinese naval and paramilitary assets at greater distances for longer periods that is visible as near constant and sustained presence in critical areas. One such instance is the recent departure of 20th task group on 3 April 2015, for anti-piracy operations off the Horn of Africa (HoA).[27] Since December 2008, China has maintained a continuous three ship deployment comprising two combatants and one replenishment ship for this tasking. In addition, the Chinese naval task groups, either enroute or on completion of their anti-piracy deployments, have visited virtually every nation bordering the Mediterranean, IOR and the Western Pacific. In certain cases, such deployments have included visits to Europe, Latin America and Oceania.[28] These can be seen as virtual 'hub and spoke' strategy for influence building using the symbolism and the attached political content besides an opportunity to display their technological prowess.

A Systemic-Regional-Bilateral Comparative Analysis

In this section, a comparative analysis of China's actions in maritime domain in the Western Pacific and the IOR is undertaken to trace the similarities and differences through a systemic-regional-bilateral perspective. In systemic global sense, China has participated in the RIMPAC series of exercises off Hawaii for the first time and signed the Conduct on Unalerted Encounters as Sea (CUES) agreement at the Western Pacific Naval Symposium (WPNS) at Qingdao, in 2014. It is also worth mention that this was also the case for India. In the IOR, as mentioned earlier, China has contributed to global antipiracy efforts since 2008 by escort operations as part of independent group, in a similar vein as India.

At the regional level, China has continued with its 'assertive' actions in the South China and East China seas. Some recent examples include

(a) Promulgation of an Air Defence Identification Zone (ADIZ) in East China Sea that overlaps with the existing Japanese ADIZ in November 2013.

(b) Positioning of its largest oil exploration platform Haiyang Shiyou 981 in the disputed waters with Vietnam in May 2014 leading to adverse reactions from Hanoi besides rioting and arson directed against Chinese business interests in Vietnam.

(c) Close quarter situations with the US Navy cruiser Cowpens in November 2013 and, P8A Poseidon Maritime Patrol aircraft in August 2014.

(d) Large-scale reclamation and development activities on islands and low lying/shallow features in the South China seas inviting opposition from the Philippines, Vietnam. Indonesia, the US and other regional stakeholders.[29]

In the IOR, a Chinese nuclear submarine was first deployed in 2013, and this was followed by two port visits to Sri Lanka by a conventional submarine and its support ship in 2014.[30] At first glance, the berthing of these naval assets seem 'perfectly legitimate' considering the fact that 'rest and replenishment' were necessary after long transit voyage through South China Sea (SCS). However, the rationale that the submarine was deployed for escort duties as part of anti-piracy operation seems 'operationally fragile', As a result, obvious negative analyses have emanated from India emphasising that there is 'much more' to this deployment than meets the eye.

At the bilateral level, Chinas proactive assertiveness in SCS and East China Sea (ECS) was mirrored in the two major standoffs in the disputed areas of the Himalayan border. The fact that these confrontations took place while the Chinese premier and the President were on official visits to India makes these significant. The observation in some quarters that these were independent and unrelated actions by the Chinese military does not seem logical. The timings and their repeated nature also obviate the possibility that these were coincidental.

In sum, there is constant thread running across the 'strategic behaviour' by China where it is ready to cooperate and contribute on issues that do not affect its s called 'core issues'.

Conclusion

In view of the above discussion, the policy responses would have to factor a mix of 'cooperation and competition' and this would extend 'within and among' the strategic dimensions of politics, economics, and security. An enhanced influence building and naval presence by China is a definite given its vital stakes in the IOR. What remains to be seen is the 'tone, tenor and temper' of its interactions and engagements in the Indian Ocean. A careful analysis of this trend becomes important for India in its renewed efforts for an inclusive, multi-sectoral and cooperative architecture. At this stage it would be worth recall the axiom that coexistence of cooperative, competitive and conflictual tendencies is an inevitability in current globalised environment.[31] Another approach could be derived by framing a reputed game theorist logic for international relations, where it is averred that most of the 'interesting strategic relationships' are, in fact variable-sum games where a single track policy of pure cooperation or absolute friction is not the optimal option.[32] In this case, selective engagement that mutates across the ambit of strategic institutions appears to be a more feasible alternative. While India may and has cooperated on some aspects like joining the Asian Infrastructure Investment Bank (AIIB) and positive response to the BCIM initiative, it has been reticent in giving support to the 'whole of MSR' project. Such dual track strategies of walking along or away by examining the 'give and take' apropos the 'pros and cons' will allow to successful management of the simultaneous paradoxes. However, this would require various shades of internal (hard) and external (collective) balancing. These would have to be supported by 'smart hedging' through implicit choices to cooperate or compete with major players. The recent articulations by the national and military leaderships indicate that such a policy framework is evolving and augurs well for taking the 'India story' forward.

Appendix A

CHINA'S REGIONAL TRADE STATISTICS 2003-2013, (constant US $ Bn for respective years)

Source: China Academies Press, *China Statistical Yearbooks*, various editions, Extracted and arranged by the author

Region	2003				2004				2005				2006			
	Total	Exports	Imports	Balance	Total	Exports	Imports	Balance	Total	Exports	Imports	Balance	Total	Exports	Imports	Balance
Global	851.0	438.2	412.8	25.5	1154.6	593.3	561.2	32.1	1421.9	762.0	660.0	102.0	1760.4	968.9	791.5	177.5
Asia	495.5	222.6	272.9	-50.3	664.9	295.5	369.4	-73.9	807.9	366.4	441.5	-75.1	981.1	455.7	525.4	-69.6
Africa	18.5	10.2	8.4	1.8	29.5	13.8	15.6	-1.8	39.7	18.7	21.1	-2.4	55.5	26.7	28.8	-2.1
Europe	157.9	88.2	69.7	18.5	211.4	122.4	89.0	33.4	262.1	165.6	96.4	69.2	330.2	215.4	114.9	100.5
Latin America	26.8	11.9	14.9	-3.1	40.0	18.2	21.8	-3.5	50.5	23.7	26.8	-3.1	70.2	36.0	34.2	1.9
North America	136.4	98.1	38.3	59.9	185.3	133.2	52.0	81.2	230.8	174.7	56.2	118.5	286.0	219.1	66.9	152.2
Oceania and Pacific Islands	15.9	7.3	8.6	-1.3	23.5	10.2	13.3	-3.2	30.9	12.9	18.0	-5.1	37.3	16.0	21.3	-5.3

Region	2007				2008				2009				2010			
	Total	Exports	Imports	Balance	Total	Exports	Imports	Balance	Total	Exports	Imports	Balance	Total	Exports	Imports	Balance
Global	2173.7	1217.8	956.0	261.8	2563.3	1430.7	1132.6	298.1	2207.5	1201.6	1005.9	195.7	2974.0	1577.8	1396.2	181.5
Asia	1187.8	567.9	619.9	-52.1	1366.7	664.1	702.6	-38.5	1172.2	568.7	603.5	-34.9	1566.9	732.0	835.0	-103.0
Africa	73.7	37.3	36.4	0.9	107.2	51.2	56.0	-4.7	91.1	47.7	43.3	4.4	127.0	60.0	67.1	7.1
Europe	427.5	287.8	139.7	148.2	511.5	343.4	168.1	175.4	426.7	264.7	162.0	102.6	573.1	355.2	217.9	137.3
Latin America	102.7	51.5	51.1	0.4	143.4	71.8	71.6	0.1	121.9	57.1	64.8	-7.7	183.6	91.8	91.8	0.0
North America	332.5	252.1	80.4	171.7	368.3	274.3	94.1	180.2	328.1	238.6	89.6	149.0	422.9	305.8	117.1	188.8
Oceania and Pacific Islands	49.5	21.1	28.4	-7.3	66.1	25.9	40.2	-14.4	67.6	24.9	42.7	-17.7	99.0	33.0	66.0	-33.0

Region	2011				2012				2013			
	Total	Exports	Imports	Balance	Total	Exports	Imports	Balance	Total	Exports	Imports	Balance
Global	3641.9	1898.4	1743.5	154.9	3867.1	2048.7	1818.4	230.3	4159.0	2209.0	1950.0	259.0
Asia	1903.1	899.0	1004.1	-105.0	2045.1	1006.8	1038.3	-31.5	2224.0	1134.1	1089.9	44.1
Africa	166.3	73.1	93.2	-20.2	198.6	85.3	113.3	-27.9	210.3	92.8	117.5	-24.7
Europe	700.7	413.6	287.2	126.4	683.1	396.4	286.7	109.7	729.9	405.7	324.2	81.6
Latin America	241.4	121.7	119.7	2.1	261.3	135.2	126.1	9.1	261.4	134.0	127.4	6.5
North America	494.4	350.1	144.3	205.7	536.3	380.1	156.2	223.9	575.5	397.8	177.7	220.2
Oceania and Pacific Islands	129.8	40.9	88.9	-48.0	136.5	44.9	91.7	-46.8	153.3	44.6	108.7	-64.1

Summary of Chinas Regional Trade (2003 – 2013)				
	Total	Exports	Imports	Balance
Global	26774.3	14346.4	12428.0	1918.4
Asia	14415.2	6912.7	7502.5	-589.8
Africa	1117.3	516.8	600.5	-83.8
Europe	5014.0	3058.4	1955.7	1102.7
Latin America	1503.1	752.9	750.2	2.7
North America	3896.6	2823.9	1072.7	1751.3
Oceanic and Pacific Islands	809.5	281.7	527.9	-246.2

Appendix B

CHINA'S IOR TRADE STATISTICS – 2011-13 (constant US $ Bn for respective years)

Source: China Academies Press, *China Statistical Yearbooks*, various editions, Extracted and arranged by the author

Country	2011				2012				2013				Trade balance 2011-13
	Total	Exports	Imports	Balance	Total	Exports	Imports	Balance	Total	Exports	Imports	Balance	
Bahrain	1.2	0.9	0.3	0.6	1.6	1.2	0.3	0.9	1.5	1.2	0.3	0.9	2.3
Bangladesh	8.3	7.8	0.4	7.4	8.4	8.0	0.5	7.5	10.3	9.7	0.6	9.1	24.0
Myanmar	6.5	4.8	1.7	3.1	7.0	5.7	1.3	4.4	10.2	7.3	2.9	4.5	12.0
India	73.9	50.5	23.4	27.2	66.5	47.7	18.8	28.9	65.4	48.4	17.0	31.5	87.5
Indonesia	60.6	29.2	31.3	-2.1	66.2	34.3	32.0	2.3	68.4	36.9	31.4	5.5	5.7
Iran	45.1	14.8	30.3	-15.6	36.5	11.6	24.9	-13.3	39.4	14.0	25.4	-11.4	-40.2
Iraq	14.3	3.8	10.4	-6.6	17.6	4.9	12.7	-7.7	24.9	6.9	18.0	-11.1	-25.5
Kuwait	11.3	2.1	9.2	-7.0	12.6	2.1	10.5	-8.4	12.3	2.7	9.6	-6.9	-22.3
Laos	1.3	0.5	0.8	-0.3	1.7	0.9	0.8	0.1	2.7	1.7	1.0	0.7	0.5
Maldives	0.1	0.1	0.0	0.1	0.1	0.1	0.0	0.1	0.1	0.1	0.0	0.1	0.3
Oman	15.9	1.0	14.9	-13.9	18.8	1.8	17.0	-15.2	22.9	1.9	21.0	-19.1	-48.2
Pakistan	10.6	8.4	2.1	6.3	12.4	9.3	3.1	6.1	14.2	11.0	3.2	7.8	20.3
Qatar	5.9	1.2	4.7	-3.5	8.5	1.2	7.3	-6.1	10.2	1.7	8.5	-6.8	-16.3
S Arabia	64.3	14.8	49.5	-34.6	73.3	18.5	54.9	-36.4	72.2	18.7	53.5	-34.7	-105.7
Sri Lanka	3.1	3.0	0.2	2.8	3.2	3.0	0.2	2.8	3.6	3.4	0.2	3.3	8.9

Country	2011				2012				2013				Trade balance 2011-13
	Total	Ex-ports	Im-ports	Bal-ance	Total	Ex-ports	Im-ports	Balance	Total	Ex-ports	Im-ports	Bal-ance	
Thailand	64.7	25.7	39.0	-13.3	69.8	31.2	38.6	-7.4	71.2	32.7	38.5	-5.8	-26.5
UAE	35.1	26.8	8.3	18.5	40.4	29.6	10.9	18.7	46.2	33.4	12.8	20.6	57.8
Yemen	4.2	1.1	3.1	-2.0	5.6	2.0	3.6	-1.6	5.2	2.1	3.1	-0.9	-4.6
Comoros	0.0	0.0	0.0	0.0	0.0	0.0	0.0	0.0	0.0	0.0	0.0	0.0	0.1
Congo	5.2	0.5	4.7	-4.2	5.1	0.5	4.6	-4.0	6.5	0.8	5.7	-4.9	-13.2
Djibouti	0.5	0.5	0.0	0.5	0.9	0.9	* 0.0	0.9	1.0	1.0	0.0	1.0	2.4
Egypt	8.8	7.3	1.5	5.8	9.5	8.2	1.3	6.9	10.2	8.4	1.9	6.5	19.2
Ethiopia	1.2	0.9	0.3	0.6	1.8	1.5	0.3	1.2	2.2	1.9	0.3	1.6	3.4
Kenya	2.4	2.4	0.1	2.3	2.8	2.8	0.1	2.7	3.3	3.2	0.1	3.2	8.2
Madagascar	0.6	0.5	0.1	0.4	0.7	0.5	0.1	0.4	0.8	0.6	0.2	0.5	1.3
Malawi	0.2	0.1	0.0	0.1	0.3	0.2	0.0	0.2	0.3	0.2	0.0	0.2	0.4
Mauritius	0.5	0.5	0.0	0.5	0.6	0.6	0.0	0.6	0.7	0.6	0.0	0.6	1.7
Mozambique	1.0	0.7	0.3	0.4	1.3	0.9	0.4	0.5	1.7	1.2	0.5	0.7	1.7
Reunion	0.1	0.1	0.0	0.1	0.1	0.1	0.0	0.1	0.1	0.1	0.0	0.1	0.4
Seychelles	0.0	0.0	0.0	0.0	0.0	0.0	0.0	0.0	0.0	0.0	0.0	0.0	0.1
Sierra Leone	0.3	0.2	0.0	0.2	0.8	0.2	0.5	-0.3	1.6	0.2	1.5	-1.3	-1.4
Somalia	0.1	0.1	0.0	0.1	0.1	0.1	0.0	0.1	0.2	0.1	0.0	0.1	0.3
South Africa	45.5	13.4	32.1	-18.7	60.0	15.3	44.7	-29.3	65.2	16.8	48.4	-31.6	-79.7
Sudan	11.5	2.0	9.5	-7.5	3.7	2.2	1.6	0.6	4.5	2.4	2.1	0.3	-6.6

Country	2011				2012				2013				Trade balance 2011-13
	Total	Ex-ports	Im-ports	Bal-ance	Total	Ex-ports	Im-ports	Balance	Total	Ex-ports	Im-ports	Bal-ance	
Tanzania	2.1	1.7	0.5	1.2	2.5	2.1	0.4	1.7	3.7	3.1	0.6	2.6	5.5
Togo	1.9	1.8	0.1	1.8	3.5	3.4	0.1	3.3	2.6	2.4	0.1	2.3	7.4
Zimbabwe	0.9	0.4	0.5	-0.1	1.0	0.4	0.6	-0.2	1.1	0.4	0.7	-0.3	-0.5
Lesotho	0.1	0.1	0.0	0.1	0.1	0.1	0.0	0.1	0.1	0.1	0.0	0.1	0.2
Eritrea	0.1	0.1	0.0	0.1	0.1	0.1	0.0	0.1	0.2	0.1	0.1	0.1	0.3
Mayotte	0.0	0.0	0.0	0.0	0.0	0.0	0.0	0.0	0.1	0.1	0.0	0.1	0.1
South Sudan	0.0	0.0	0.0	0.0	0.5	0.0	0.5	-0.5	2.5	0.1	2.5	-2.4	-2.9

Summary

	Total	Exports	Imports	Balance	Total	Exports	Imports	Balance	Total	Exports	Imports	Balance	Trade balance
Global Total	3641.9	1898.4	1743.5	154.9	3867.1	2048.7	1818.4	230.3	4159.0	2209.0	1950.0	259.0	644.2
TOTAL IOR	675.7	303.1	372.7	-69.6	744.1	338.7	405.4	-66.8	799.8	371.0	428.8	-57.8	-194.2
IOR ASIA	426.4	196.6	229.7	-33.1	450.0	212.9	237.1	-24.2	481.0	234.1	246.9	-12.7	-124.1
IOR AFRICA	249.3	106.4	142.9	-36.5	294.1	125.8	168.4	-42.6	318.8	136.8	181.9	-45.1	-70.0
%AGE CONTRIBUTION IOR	18.6	16.0	21.4		19.2	16.5	22.3		19.2	16.8	22.0		

Notes and References

1   ASEAN-China Centre, "Speech by Chinese President Xi Jinping to Indonesian Parliament", 3 October 2013, http://www.aseanchinacenter.org/english/201310/03/c_133062675.htm, (accessed 17 March 2015).

2   "Xi suggests China, C. Asia build Silk Road economic belt" in *Xinhua*, 07 September 2013, http://news.xinhuanet.com/english/china/201309/ 07/c_132700695.htm, 07 Sep 2013, (accessed 17 March 2015).

3   "Xi pledges great renewal of Chinese nation" in *Xinhua*, 29 November 2012, http://news.xinhuanet.com/english/china/201309/07/c_132700695.htm, (accessed 17 March 2015).

4   "Chronology of China's "Belt and Road" initiatives "in *Xinhua*, 05 February, 2015,   http://news.xinhuanet.com/english/china/201502/05/c_133972101. htm, (accessed 17 March 2015).

5   See, Justin Yifu Lin (former Chief Economist of the World Bank), "Industry transfer to Africa good for all" in *China Daily USA*, 20 January 2015, http://usa. chinadaily.com.cn/epaper/201501/20/content_19357725.htm. For developing narrative on this theme see, Cheng Lu, "Return of maritime Silk Road does not forget Africa" in *Xinhua*, 12 February 2015, http://news.xinhuanet.com/english/indepth/2015-02/12/c_133990475.htm and, He Wenping "One Belt, One Road' can find place for Africa" in *Global Times*, 29 January 2015) in *Global Times*, http://www.globaltimes.cn/content/904823.shtml, (all accessed 21 March 2015).

6   "China unveils action plan on Belt and Road Initiative" in *Xinhua*, 28 March 2015,   http://www.china.org.cn/china/201503/28/content_35181779.htm, (accessed 29 March 2015). This entry was removed and replaced by more detailed but anodyne statement without the map on 30 March 2015.

7   For more details on the concepts of maritimity, continentality and their relevance while analysing geopolitical and strategic trends, see Saul Bernard Cohen, *Geopolitics: the Geography of International Relations* (Third Edition), (Maryland: Rowman & Littlefield, 2015), pp. 41-47.

8   James A Nathan and James K Oliver, *The Future of United States Naval Power*, (Bloomington: Indiana University Press, 1979), pp. 7-9.

9   Xinhua, Note 4.

10   Stephen Roskill, *The Strategy of Sea Power. Its Development and Application. Based on the Lees-Knowles Lectures Delivered in the University of Cambridge, 1961.* (London: Collins, 1963), pp. 15-23.

11 The majority of Chinese and Indian description of Admiral Zheng He voyages to the Indian Ocean, and that of Chola expeditions to South East Asia are projected in benign light dilating on the cultural, trade and ideational exchanges with no territory being conquered. However, sources that are more contemporary have highlighted the expeditionary streak, the use of force for extracting the acquiescence and regular payment of tribute by the indigenous rulers in a vassal-suzerain (formal inequality) manner. For example see, Geoff Wade, 'The Zheng He Voyages: A Reassessment', October 2004, Working Paper Series No. 31, Asia Research Institute; Louise Levathes, *When China Ruled the Seas: The Treasure Fleet of the Dragon Throne 1405–1433*, (New York: Simon & Schuster, 1994.), pp. 115-120, 170-175; George W. Spencer, *The Politics of Expansion - The Chola Conquest of Sri Lanka and Sri Vijaya*, (Madras: New Era, 1983), pp. 107-123, 140-145.

12 For the tripolar argument about 'Guns-Butter-Socio-economic future' framework, see, Paul M. Kennedy, *The Rise and Fall of the Great Powers: Economic Change and Military Conflict from 1500 to 2000*. (London: Unwin Hyman, 1990), pp. 444-446. See, Ramses Amer, Ashok Swain, and Joakim O jendal, *The Security-Development Nexus - Peace, Conflict and Development*, (London: Anthem Press, 2012).

13 For, a well-argued book on 'Guns versus Butter' debate see, Mary Kaldor, *The Baroque Arsenal*, (London: Abacus, 1983). For ongoing debate on the economic interdependence debate see, Edward D. Mansfield, and Brian Pollins, *Economic Interdependence and International Conflict New Perspectives on an Enduring Debate* (Ann Arbor: University of Michigan Press, 2006). For a historical overview covering the past two hundred years and the changing dynamics of economics-security nexus, see, Dale C Copeland, *Economic Interdependence and War*, (Princeton: Princeton University Press, 2014).

14 George Modelski and William R. Thompson. *Seapower in Global Politics, 1494-1993*, (Seattle: University of Washington Press, 1988), pp. 11-18.

15 Wolfgang Wegener, *The Naval Strategy of the World War*, (Annapolis, Md: Naval Institute Press, 1989), pp. 31-38 and, Herbert Rosinski, *The Development of Naval Thought: Essays*. (Newport, R.I.: Naval War College Press, 1977), pp. 59-63.

16 Yves-Heng Lim, *China's Naval Power: An Offensive Realist Approach*. Farnham, (Surrey: Ashgate, 2014).

17 Robert Harkavy has penned two excellent books on the theme of the differing approaches adopted and the various basing options employed through the course of history. These are, *Great Power Competition for Overseas Bases: The*

Geopolitics of Access Diplomacy, (New York: Pergamon Press, 1982) and, *Bases Abroad: The Global Foreign Military Presence*, (Oxford: Oxford University Press, 1989). For the origin of 'String of Pearls' theory, see, Juli A. MacDonald, Amy Donahue, and Bethany Danyluk, *Energy Futures in Asia: Perspectives of India's Energy Security Strategy and Policies* (Washington, DC: Booz Allen Hamilton, November 2004), p. iii.

18 Desmond Ball, 'Arms and Affluence: Military Acquisitions in the Asia-Pacific Region', *International Security*, Vol. 18, No. 3 (Winter, 1993-1994), pp. 78-112, and, Robert S. Ross, 'China's Naval Nationalism: Sources, Prospects, and the U.S. Response' *International Security*, Vol. 34, No. 2 (Fall 2009), pp. 46–81.

19 Jakub J. Grygiel, *Great Powers and Geopolitical Change*, (Baltimore, Md: Johns Hopkins University Press, 2011), pp. 21-23.

20   Klaus Solberg Søilen, *Geoeconomics*, (London: Bookboon, 2012), electronic edition.

21   See, Annual Reports for 2014 by the International Monetary Fund and World Bank.

22 For negative narratives, see, Dambisa Moyo, *Winner Take All: China's Race for Resources and What It Means for the World* (New York: Basic Books, 2012) and, Elizabeth Economy and Michael A. Levi, *By All Means Necessary: How China's Resource Quest Is Changing the World*, (New York: Oxford University Press. 2014). The favourable discourse on this issue can be found in Ann Lee, *What the U.S. Can Learn from China - An Open-Minded Guide to Treating Our Greatest Competitor As Our Greatest Teacher* (San Francisco: Berrett-Koehler, 2012); Theodore H. Moran, *China's Strategy to Secure Natural Resources Risks, Dangers, and Opportunities* (Washington, DC: Peterson Institute for International Economics, 2010), and; Edward S .Steinfeld, *Playing Our Game: Why China's Economic Rise Doesn't Threaten the West*, (Oxford: Oxford University Press, 2010).

23 United States Office of the Secretary of Defense, Annual Report to Congress, *Military and Security Developments Involving the People's Republic of China 2014*, p. 7, and; Congressional Research Service Report # RL33153, *China Naval Modernization: Implications for U.S. Navy Capabilities—Background and Issues for Congress*, 23 December 2014, pp. 18-20.

24 Compiled from various annual editions of IHS Group, *Janes Fighting Ships* and IISS, *Military Balance*.

25 IHS Janes, *Defence Budgets - China*, August 2014, copyrighted material, used with permission.

26   Raghavendra Mishra, 'String of Pearls and Beyond: Chinese Influence in South Asian Littoral' in KK Agnihotri and Gurpreet S Khurana (Eds), *Maritime Power Building: New 'Mantra' for China's Rise*, (New Delhi: Pentagon Press, 2015), pp. 53-55, and; Pieter D. Wezeman and Siemon T. Wezeman, 'Trends in International Arms transfers', SIPRI Fact Sheet, March 2015, http://books.sipri.org/files/FS/SIPRIFS1503.pdf, (accessed 04 April 2015).

27   "China Sends New Anti-Piracy Mission to Gulf of Aden", *Associated Press, Beijing*, 3 April 2015, http://abcnews.go.com/International/wireStory/china-sends-anti-piracy-mission-gulf-aden-30079706, (accessed 03 April 2015).

28   Kamlesh K. Agnihotri, *Strategic Direction of the Chinese Navy: Capability and Intent Assessment*, (New Delhi: Bloomsbury, 2015), pp. 126-129.

29   For a recent report about such activities, see, James Hardy and Sean O'Connor, 'China starts work on Mischief Reef land reclamation', 11 March 2015, *IHS Jane's Defence Weekly*, http://www.janes.com/article/49917/china-starts-work-on-mischief-reef-land-reclamation, (accessed 04 April 2015).

30   In February 2014, the Director of the U.S. Defense Intelligence Agency (DIA) confirmed that China had "recently deployed for the first time a nuclear powered attack submarine to the Indian Ocean." For more details, see Michael T. Flynn, "Defense Intelligence Agency Annual Threat Assessment: Statement Before the Senate Armed Services Committee, United States Senate", 11 February 2014, www.dia.mil/Portals/27/Documents/News/2014_DIA_SFR_SASC_ATA_FINAL.pdf. Also, Shihar Aneez and Ranga Sirilal, "Chinese submarine docks in Sri Lanka despite Indian concerns", *Reuters*, 2 November 2014, http://in.reuters.com/article/2014/11/02/sri-lanka-china-submarine-idINKBN0IM0LU20141102, and; Atul Aneja, "China says its submarine docked in Sri Lanka 'for replenishment'", *The Hindu,* 28 November 2014, http://www.thehindu.com/news/international/world/china-says-its-submarine-docked-in-sri-lanka-for-replenishment/article6643129.ece, (all accessed 04 April 2015).

31   Geoffrey Till, *Seapower: A Guide for the Twenty-First Century*, (New York: Routledge, 2009), p. 16-18.

32   Thomas Schelling, *The Strategy of Conflict*, (Massachusetts: Harvard University Press, 1981), p. 4-8.

4 | Southeast Asian Responses to China's 21ˢᵗ Century Maritime Silk Road Initiative

Irene Chan

In merely three decades, China has gained geo-economic dominance and became the undisputed driver of growth for many Asian countries. However, China's rise has inevitably been seen as a threat to existing regional order. Its pledge of a peaceful rise failed to gain traction with its neighbours, particularly those in Southeast Asia, due to mistrust and tensions arising from territorial disputes. Therefore, when China's fifth generation leaders came into power in 2013, they formulated proactive initiatives to address the country's fundamental foreign policy dilemma. In order to create a favourable external environment for domestic growth, the new leadership under Xi Jinping and Li Keqiang mounted new diplomatic initiatives, including the much publicized One Belt, One Road initiative (also known as the Belt Road Initiative or BRI) which is based on the concept of reviving the ancient Chinese land and maritime networks of trade routes.

A month after the announcement of the Silk Road Economic Belt (SREB) initiative for Central Asia, China's President Xi Jinping put forth the Maritime Silk Road of the 21ˢᵗ Century (MSR) proposal for Southeast Asia in his speech to the Indonesian parliament during his official visit in October 2013. Xi pointed out that China and Southeast Asian countries have found their own unique development paths. Regional countries should respect and support one another in pursuit of economic and social development to improve people's lives.[1]

He offered to widen China's doors to Southeast Asian countries so as to allow them to reap more spill-over benefits from its continued development. Beijing will strengthen cooperation with regional countries, "with a view to jointly seizing opportunities and meeting challenges for the benefit of common development and prosperity."[2] In particular, Xi committed China to greater connectivity with the region and proposed the establishment of an Asian Infrastructure Investment Bank (AIIB) that would give priority to Southeast Asia's development needs.[3]

It is an understatement to say that Southeast Asia is important to China since ancient times. Besides straddling some of the most crucial maritime trade routes in the world, the region is a source of raw materials, and a market for China's goods and services. It is also home to the intractable South China Sea disputes. In order to maintain peace on China's periphery and create a favourable environment for domestic growth, Beijing has made Southeast Asia is an integral part of its new proactive Silk Road diplomacy. This paper is an attempt to answer the following questions on the MSR:

- What is ASEAN's response to and concerns of the MSR?

- How can we explain Southeast Asian countries' varied responses to the MSR?

- Will the different needs and perceptions of Southeast Asian countries affect the China's considerations for the MSR?

China and Southeast Asian countries have to work closely on the bilateral and multilateral levels so as to implement the MSR. Therefore, it is crucial to examine the regional responses to the MSR, so as to analyze the potential contributions that the successful implementation of the MSR may bring and the challenges China faces during the process of negotiation and implementation.

This paper is based on an the initial research findings from an on-going research project on the BRI carried out by the China Programme with the Institute of Defence and Strategic Studies in the S. Rajaratnam School of International Studies. The project members travelled to two different regions, namely Central Asia and Southeast Asia, to conduct interviews with government officials and local scholars so as to gain a better understanding of the local responses to the BRI. The analysis will also be supported by secondary data such as media reports, expert commentaries, and official statements from local leadership.

Broad Overview of Existing Narrative

A review of the literature would show that although the BRI is a relatively new initiative, some scholars have done initial analysis from strategic, geopolitical and economic viewpoints. For instance, Morgan Clemens argues that the Chinese flag may follow its increasing trade relations with neighbouring countries under the MSR initiative, particularly in South Asia. He attributes his argument to the Chinese navy's strategic motivations in expanding its military presence in the Indian Ocean but stresses that, in the long run, "there is very little inevitability concerning the expansion of China's military presence along the Maritime Silk Road" as China faces major capacity and financial constraints in expanding its military presence west of Singapore.

In writing about China's BRI, David Arase points out how China's approach to regional integration is different from ASEAN-style regionalism and that smaller countries around China will likely face its power and authority without the protection of the full range of international legal norms and institutions when they have a dispute with China. He also argues that China will be prepared to use force to protect its core interests, especially its territorial sovereignty and claims. However, a critical question he does not address the issue on how varied responses that ASEAN member countries have displayed towards the MSR may potentially affect any attempts on China's part to run the initiative like a one-man show. Another scholar, Rajeev R. Chaturvedy, briefly touches upon ASEAN interests and responses towards the MSR in his working paper. He points out that in general, regional countries acknowledge the potential benefits they may reap from improved regional connectivity.

The Chinese literature on the MSR in Southeast Asia is generally positive. Chinese scholars and analysts see the MSR as a means to reduce tensions brought about by the intractable South China Sea disputes.[4] It should be noted that there are scholars who advocate a cautious and carefully researched approach to pursuing the MSR. According to Xue Li, a China-based scholar, Beijing has to consider three important factors in order for the new initiative to work: (1) the US rebalancing strategy; (2) responses from regional countries; (3) financial and political risks.[5] The fact that Beijing is indeed mindful of the receptivity and responses from regional countries is underscored by the multiple fact-finding delegations that the Chinese Ministry of Foreign Affairs, think tanks and provincial governments have sent out to various ASEAN countries, such as Indonesia, Singapore, and Thailand.[6]

ASEAN's Response

At the 17th China-ASEAN Summit in November 2013, Chinese Prime Minister Li Keqiang put forward a "2+7 Cooperation Framework" for building a community of shared destiny, of which the MSR is a part of. It comprises a two-point political consensus on building strategic trust, and promoting mutually beneficial economic development as well as seven priority areas for cooperation that include maritime cooperation, finance, security, environmental protection and people-to-people exchange.[7] Under the framework, China proposed to improve upon the China-ASEAN Free Trade Agreement; establish the Asian Infrastructure Investment Bank; and enhance China-ASEAN financial cooperation. ASEAN countries' responses to the economic components of the 2+7 Cooperation Framework was generally positive. However, this did not translate into an official endorsement of the MSR.[8]

The MSR dovetails with ASEAN's ongoing efforts to enhance physical connectivity across the region. ASEAN's collective wish to sustain the economic competitiveness of the region and to provide a foundation for continued peace and prosperity in Asia resulted in the endorsement of the ASEAN Connectivity initiative in October 2009 and the adoption of the Master Plan on ASEAN Connectivity (MPAC) a year later. The MPAC has identified 15 priority projects for physical, institutional and people-to-people connectivity. However, not all initiatives under the MPAC will be applicable in the MSR initiative. At this stage, ASEAN is unclear if China will seek to link its ongoing connectivity initiatives, where applicable, into the MSR.

With greater tensions arising from China's massive land reclamation in the South China Sea, it is unlikely that ASEAN will issue an official endorsement of the MSR as it is difficult to gain a unanimous support for it. The ASEAN countries' varied responses to the MSR will be discussed in the following section. At the point of writing, there is no unified response or official endorsement from ASEAN to the MSR even though ASEAN has acknowledged China's attempts to promote it at the various multilateral meetings.[9]

However, there have been instances where ASEAN's acknowledgements of China's MSR promotion were reported in the Chinese media as a collective endorsement of the MSR. For example, Xinhua reported on the "wide understanding, support and positive response from the participating ASEAN ministers" at the 13th ASEAN Economic Ministers-the Chinese Ministry of Commerce (AEM-MOFCOM) Consultations in August 2014.[10] In another recent instance, the Chinese Ambassador to Brunei was quoted in a news report saying that ASEAN was wise to have made the collective decision to join the AIIB.[11] Although all ten ASEAN member countries are approved founding members of the AIIB, each country's decision to join is more likely driven by self interests than the result of regional consensus. This was underscored by the fact that there was no mention of the AIIB in the Chairman's Statement for the 26th Summit regarding the discussion of the Initiative for ASEAN Integration, which deals with the economic development gaps in the region.[12]

China seems to be satisfied with its interpretation of ASEAN's response to the MSR at the moment. In the BRI's vision and action plan, Beijing clearly indicated that the MSR will be implemented mainly through bilateral cooperation. Beijing has identified ASEAN as a multilateral platform for promotional and communication purposes.[13] In addition, China has also proposed to establish an separate international summit forum for the BRI.

Regional Concerns

In a commentary, Bilahari Kausikan, the former Permanent Secretary of the Ministry of Foreign Affairs of Singapore, pointed out that "The asymmetry of the relationship [between China and ASEAN countries] can only become more salient as China grows. The various projects under the "2+7 Cooperation Framework", burgeoning ASEAN-China trade, and Chinese investments in infrastructure are binding South-western China and Southeast Asia into one economic and hence one strategic and political space. The benefits are clear and to be welcomed. But at the same time, fundamental concepts of inter-state relations are being modified. ... The forces of globalization, the many planned ASEAN-China projects, and initiatives like the new maritime silk route are re-establishing historical patterns in new ways and adding new layers of complexity to even the most positive of relationships."[14]

In a region where autonomy is highly valued, ASEAN's asymmetric relationship with China is a rising concern.[15] The question of finding a balance of autonomy in the evolving ASEAN-China relationship has to be addressed eventually.[16] In particular, ASEAN member countries fear that economic overdependence on China will erode their autonomy in making foreign policies.[17] This fear was realised in 2012 when Cambodia was deemed to have been pressured by its biggest investor and trading partner to shape the agenda in its favour.[18] It resulted in ASEAN's unprecedented failure to issue a joint communiqué.[19] There is also a fear of China's arbitrary style as the dominant power. Rule of law is hardly China's strong suit. It has been pointed out that China's approach to regional integration through the OBOR is different from ASEAN-style regionalism and that smaller countries around China will likely face its power and authority without the protection of the full range of international legal norms and institutions when they have a dispute with China.[20]

While this should not be taken literally to mean that China will behave with utter disregard to international law, it is a valid concern on regional countries' part, which China has to consider. For instance, in August 2013 after the Philippines filed its arbitration case against China, Beijing allegedly cancelled President Benigno Aquino's invitation to the 10th China-ASEAN Expo in Nanning, even though the country was designated as the country of honour for the year.[21] Again, in November 2014, a Wall Street Journal report speculated that the Philippines would be excluded from the MSR because of its legal challenge to China's South China Sea claims. The Philippines' Foreign Undersecretary for Economic Relations, Ms Laura del Rosario, was quoted saying that the Philippines felt it was left out of the plan.[22]

While many ASEAN member countries are upbeat with deepening economic ties with China, they remain cautious with regards to China's political and security enhancement proposals under the 2+7 Cooperation Framework. ASEAN's strategic concerns remain in spite of China's economic charm offensive. After all, railways, roads and ports have historical importance as integrative, political and strategic forces. Observers have argued that control of sea lines and strategic egress is increasingly pertinent to China's strategic designs on Southeast Asia and on the Indian Ocean.[23] Under the euphoria of China's exciting new initiative, regional scholars and diplomats are raising the following questions on regional security - what are China's deeper motivations behind the initiative? What roles will the Chinese navy and maritime law enforcement agencies eventually play in the MSR?[24]

Littoral ASEAN countries' lack of strategic trust in China has been played up by incidences such as the deployment of the Haiyang Shiyou 982 oil rig in disputed waters off the Paracel Islands in May 2014 and its large-scale land reclamation in the Spratly Islands. The latter is a particularly sensitive issue as it is argued that the construction of landing strips across the disputed waters could easily be used for military purposes. China did not to address the South China Sea disputes in the political and security components in the 2+7 Cooperation Framework, under which the MSR falls. Beijing has steadfastly rejected attempts by ASEAN countries to manage the disputes as well. This refusal continues to raise doubts of China's claim that it would to separate a purely economic initiative from its political and security motivations.

Select ASEAN members' responses

It took Beijing more than 18 months to formulate an official vision and action plan for the BRI, which was unveiled at the 2015 Boao Forum on 28 March. The resulting lack of clarity, unfortunately for China, gave rise to speculation and suspicion among the countries in Southeast Asia. The responses from 10 ASEAN members can be divided into the categories as shown in Figure 1.

Figure 1. Response to MSR from ASEAN

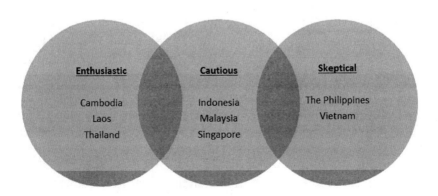

Source: Author's Interpretation

The general response from individual Southeast Asian countries is that they agree in principle to China's MSR proposal, given that China is a key economic partner and investor with deep pockets. Based on this rationale, all ten members of the Association of Southeast Asian Nations (ASEAN) have signed on as founding members of the new Asian Infrastructure Investment Bank (AIIB). The leaders of many ASEAN member countries have been reported to be supportive of the MSR either by Chinese or international media. For instance, Singapore's Prime Minister Lee Hsien Loong , Myanmar

As some of the ASEAN member countries are embroiled in the South China Sea disputes with China, it is hardly surprising that there will be mixed responses from Southeast Asian countries. Some have voiced their full support for the MSR, while others have adopted a cautious stance.

Our field research in ASEAN countries such as Singapore, Indonesia, Vietnam, Malaysia and Thailand showed that while these countries welcome Chinese initiatives to boost regional infrastructure development, they prefer to wait for further information from China before making the decision to sign any accords on the MSR trade network. Although the political leaders from Singapore, Malaysia and Indonesia have officially endorsed the MSR, their governments are quietly cautious about giving China carte blanche in the MSR.

Brief country analysis will be presented in this section on the domestic and strategic responses of each country towards the MSR.

Thailand

In comparison with the rest of the countries in our study, Thailand appears to be more enthusiastic towards the MSR. The Kingdom's response to the Chinese initiative is important due to the close Sino-Thai relationship and Thailand's position as an influential player in mainland Southeast Asia. Thailand and China have forged a special relationship since the late 1970s. Both countries had formed a de facto strategic alliance during the 1978-9 Cambodian crisis. Thailand played a vital role in bridging Sino-ASEAN relations during the period.

Given that successive Thai administrations have been trying to raise the country as the rail and road hub of mainland Southeast Asia, Beijing's MSR proposal is a boon to realizing Bangkok's infrastructure-led growth.[25]

However, the greatest hurdle to realizing this dream is the Kingdom's fracture politics. Domestic political instability has not only affected foreign investment and economic development in Thailand, but also its relations with the two key players in the region – the US and China. Washington's criticism of the coup seems to be pushing the junta closer to Beijing.[26]

Bangkok welcomes Beijing's flexibility in negotiating deals that cater to its unique needs. In particular, the Thais appreciate China's flexibility in handling bilateral agreements which have been affected by the political instability. Despite the political instability in Thailand, both countries signed two Memorandums of Understanding (MoU) on railway cooperation and cooperation in agricultural products trade on 19 December 2014. It should be noted that the MoU on railway cooperation has been subsumed under China's grand plan to create a modern Silk Road on mainland Southeast Asia. Infrastructure projects in Thailand are facing difficulties as a two-trillion-baht loan bill proposed by the Yingluck administration was been derailed by the Thai Constitutional Court.[27] Much of the funding from the bill was earmarked for transport infrastructure projects. However, even though the junta has approved in principle Thailand's joining of the AIIB, it is a caretaker administration and it is not immediately clear if it was legal for the junta to conclude any stance on the AIIB set-up.

Although Thailand is a US treaty ally, Bangkok is facing strong US criticism for the May 2014 military coup. The current US-Thai relations have deteriorated after top US envoy for East Asia, Daniel Russel, rebuked the ruling junta in January 2015. This also caused the Obama administration to scale down on the annual Cobra Gold exercises, suspend aid and cancel some exchanges with Thailand. Analysts have pointed out that the US has alienated its long time ally and pushed Thailand into China's embrace. Both Thailand and China have since stepped up military relations.[28]

However, Thailand remains cautious in maintaining the balance of power by drawing closer to Japan. After visiting China in December 2014, Thai Prime Minister Prayut visited Japan in February 2015 and sought to strengthen bilateral economic relations and bolster his regime legitimacy.[29] Japan is one of Thailand's major investors but the domestic political instability has resulted in a 37 percent drop in Japanese investments in 2014.[30] Thailand and Japan have signed an MOU for the East-West Corridor rail link on 27 May 2015, after Japan signalled its intention to compete with China for Asian infrastructure development by unveiling a US$110 billion aid plan.[31]

Vietnam

Although Vietnam is a founding member of the AIIB, it has not given an official endorsement of the MSR. In fact, Vietnamese Prime Minister Nguyen Tan Dung, questioned China's deeper motivations behind the MSR in an article on his official blog.[32] Vietnam is highly suspicious of the MSR proposal due to the Haiyang Shiyou 981 oilrig standoff near the disputed Paracel Islands in May 2014. Relations between Beijing and Hanoi sank to an all time low during the standoff. Although both parties have made efforts to normalize relations, Vietnam remains skeptical of Chinese economic advances without addressing the South China Sea disputes. In my interviews with Vietnamese scholars and officials, they highlighted the lack of clarity of the MSR initiative and insufficient consultation with Vietnam even though Hanoi was identified on the map as a stop. The Vietnamese are extremely skeptical towards the initiatives that China is undertaking towards its neighbors.

In July 2014, reports emerged that the coastal cities of Guangzhou, Hainan, Zhanjiang, Beihai, Quanzhou, Zhangzhou, Ningbo, Penglai and Yangzhou made a joint proposal pushing for UNESCO World Heritage recognition of the ancient MSR. Chinese reports also claim that the cultural heritage authorities have conducted frequent archeological surveys of the Paracel Islands and are expanding the surveys southwards to the Spratly Islands. This raised concerns, particularly from Vietnam, that China may use the MSR as a way to reinstate its historical presence in the region and legitimise their increased presence and fortifications of its claims in the South China Sea.

Malaysia

China has long perceived Malaysia as a moderate claimant in the South China Sea, along with Brunei. Beijing was silent when Malaysia and Brunei signed agreements for joint development of offshore blocks in waters that fall within China's nine dashed lines in 2013.[33] Malaysia reciprocated by warmly supporting the MSR proposal. "Cooperation in the establishment of the 21st Century Maritime Silk Road was incorporated into the Joint Communiqué between Malaysia and China in conjuncion with the 40th anniversary of diplomatic relations in May 2014. Malaysian Transport Minister, Dato' Sri Liow Tiong Lai, has repeatedly expressed Malaysia's support for the 21st Century Maritime Silk Road. ... And last month, Prime

Minister Najib [Razak] reiterated that Malaysia supported the initiative in principle and was getting further details from China."[34] However, the South China Sea dispute remains as a challenge between Malaysia and China. As the Chairman of ASEAN in 2015, Malaysia issued a strong message on the land reclamation activities in South China Sea. While Malaysia's positions on the South China Sea disputes and the MSR have not changed, the country has shown that its moderation and support should not be seen as giving a carte blanche to China.

Meanwhile, Malaysia has sought to build closer relations with the US and Japan. It elevated relations with the United States to the status of Comprehensive Partnership in 2014.[35] The growing cooperation between US and Malaysian militaries was highlighted by the 2014 Cooperation Afloat Readiness and Training (CARAT) Malaysia exercise between the US Navy and the Royal Malaysian Navy; and the MALUS Amphex 2014 between the US Marine Corps and the Malaysian Armed Forces, which took place in Eastern Sabah.[36] Malaysia also sought US assistance to build a MAF marine type unit for rapid response, based on the US Marine Corps model.[37] Malaysia has further sought to diversify its strategic relations by elevating bilateral relations with Japan to a strategic partnership amidst recent tensions in the South China Sea. In the joint statement issued after the meeting, both countries reaffirmed the importance of maintaining peace, stability, security and freedom of navigation in and over-flight over the South China Sea.[38]

Singapore

Singapore holds pragmatic views of the MSR proposal from the economic standpoint, rather than through a geopolitical or strategic approach. In interviews with Chinese media in 2014, Singapore Prime Minister Lee Hsien Loong stated that Singapore welcomes China's efforts to develop relations with ASEAN countries, including the MSR proposal.[39] He commented that Singapore stands to benefit from the new opportunities arising from greater regional connectivity as it is as a major transportation, logistics and maritime hub.[40]

In personal interviews with various Singaporean scholars and former diplomats revealed that as the only advanced economy in Southeast Asia, Singapore faces certain pressure from other ASEAN countries to provide greater assistance to boost regional infrastructure connectivity, even though its ability to provide assistance is limited due to its small size. If successful, China's AIIB, Silk Road Fund and MSR will be able to relieve some of the pressure on Singapore. After careful consideration, Singapore became the first advanced economy to sign on as a founding member of the AIIB.

Singapore is not a South China Sea claimant but it understands that the disputes have presented a grave challenge to improving regional connectivity. Therefore, Singapore has made repeated calls for all parties involved to remain calm during times of great tension and to seek the early conclusion of the Code of Conduct under the ASEAN framework.[41] Former Foreign Minister, George Yeo, also made calls to regional countries to put the South China Sea disputes in perspective and work with China to "realize this potential for unprecedented prosperity."[42]

Indonesia

As the biggest ASEAN country, Indonesia undoubtedly plays a major role in China's MSR.[43] Xi chose Indonesia as the first stop for his inaugural Southeast Asia visit in October 2013. His visit marked a new chapter in Indonesia-China relations as bilateral cooperation was elevated from strategic partnership to comprehensive strategic partnership. Most importantly, it was during the visit to Jakarta that the MSR was first introduced to the region. Indonesia welcomed the idea of the MSR but it remained cautious due to the lack of clarity from China. Indonesia was also preoccupied with domestic elections in 2014 and did not pursue the MSR actively.

Analysts have noted the emergence of Indonesia's maritime aspirations during the 2014 electoral debates where Indonesia President Joko Widodo, more popularly known as Jokowi, promised in his election manifesto to strengthen Indonesia's maritime security and to project the Indonesian navy as a respected regional maritime power in East Asia.[44] Jokowi announced his signature maritime fulcrum doctrine at the East Asia Summit (EAS) in November 2014 and sought to link it with the MSR.[45] Talks between Indonesian and Chinese foreign ministers on the sidelines of the EAS also revealed Indonesia's expectation to be viewed by China as an equal.[46]

In spite of its belated entry to the AIIB, Indonesia is seeking to play a major role in the new China-led international bank. This move was warmly welcomed by China and Beijing has pledged to invest US$50 billion in Indonesian infrastructure projects.[47] However, due to the past experience with low level of realisation of Chinese investment plans, Indonesia is taking precautions to push Chinese investors and to attract other external investors such as Japan, Korea and the European Union countries.[48]

Indonesia has concerns regarding overlapping Chinese claims in its exclusive economic zone but it has clearly stated that it is not a claimant in the South China Sea disputes. Jakarta has been seeking to be a leading mediator in the matter. However, a close relationship between China and Indonesia may trigger intra-ASEAN anxiety. The interviews with regional scholars have reflected some concern for this issue. They attribute it to the fact that ASEAN countries are unwilling for Indonesia to be their representative in the South China Sea issue or in the MSR, although the latter is the biggest country amongst the ASEAN members.

Conclusion

At the end of the day, the smaller countries feel that they may have more to lose if they do not go onboard China's MSR initiative. Interviews with analysts, scholars and government officials from the various ASEAN countries reflect a general sentiment that China's rise is unstoppable and no country in this region would like to incur Chinese disfavour unnecessarily. There is an ever present fear of losing out, or being left out of the region's economic progress. On the other hand, ASEAN countries are not willing to subsume their foreign policy making autonomy under Chinese influence. They are also wary of Chinese military ambitions. Therefore, the majority of Southeast Asian countries will continue to seek to hedge against China by boosting their strategic relations with China's perceived rivals – the US, Japan and India.

Notes and References

1   'Speech by Chinese President Xi Jinping to Indonesian Parliament -ASEAN-China Center', *Asean-china-center.org*, http://www.asean-china-center.org/english/2013-10/03/c_133062675.htm, (accessed 14 April 2015).

2   Ibid.

3   Ibid.

4   Jiang Zhida , 'ASEAN will gain from Maritime Silk Road', *China Institute of International Studies*, http://www.ciis.org.cn/english/2015-03/31/content_7790236.htm; 'How China Can Perfect Its 'Silk Road' Strategy', *The Diplomat*, http://thediplomat.com/2015/04/how-china-can-perfect-its-silk-road-strategy/; 'Maritime Silk Road key to joint development', *Global Times*, http://www.globaltimes.cn/content/889599.shtml; (all accessed 25 April 2015).

5   Ftchinese.com (2015). "一带一路"折射的中国外交风险 – 评论 - *FT中文网* Retrieved 12 March 2015, from http://www.ftchinese.com/story/001059886.

6   The author participated in two roundtable discussions with such fact-finding delegations sent out by the Guangdong and Guangxi provincial governments in 2014. Interviews with Indonesian analysts also revealed that the Chinese Embassy in Jakarta was engaged in an in-depth study with a prominent think tank for Indonesia's responses on the MSR. However, results of the study were not publicly released for unspecified reasons.

7   Chairman's Statement of the 17th ASEAN-China Summit, Nay Pyi Taw, Myanmar, 13 November 2014, Paragraph 6.

8   Prashanth Parameswaran, 'Beijing Unveils New Strategy for ASEAN–China Relations', http://www.jamestown.org/single/?tx_ttnews%5Btt_news%5D=41526&no_cache=1#.VXAgomCJgdU, (accessed 25 April 2015).

9   Note 7 Ibid, Paragraph 4 and; Joint Media Statement of the 13th AEM-MOFCOM Consultations, Nay Pyi Taw, Myanmar, 26 August 2014, Paragraph 5.

10 'ASEAN economic ministers seek to form new maritime silk route jointly', Xinhua News Agency, 27 August 2014, http://news.xinhuanet.com/english/china/2014-08/27/c_133590715.htm, (accessed 22 April 2015).

11 Quratul-Ain Bandial, 'Good relations crucial to maritime silk road: Yang Jian', *The Brunei Times*, http://www.bt.com.bn/news-national/2015/04/25/good-

relations-crucial-maritime-silk-road-yang-jian, (accessed 03 May 2015).

12 Entry by Edmund Sim, 'Wrap-up of the 26th ASEAN Summit', *AEC Blog*, http://aseanec.blogspot.sg/2015/04/wrap-up-of-26th-asean-summit.html, (accessed 10 May 2015).

13 'Full Text: Vision and actions on jointly building Belt and Road', *Xinhua| English.news.cn*, http://news.xinhuanet.com/english/china/2015-03/28/c_ 134105858.htm, (accessed 30 March 2015).

14 Bilahari Kausikan, 'ASEAN-China Relations: Building a Common Destiny?', *The American Interest*, http://www.the-american-interest.com/2014/09/23/ asean-china-relations-building-a-common-destiny/, (accessed 01 February 2015).

15 Simon Tay, 'China, ASEAN at Crossroads', *The Japan Times* , http://www. japantimes.co.jp/opinion/2013/08/15/commentary/world-commentary/ china-asean-at-crossroads/, (accessed on 01 May 2015); also cited in Prashanth Parameswaran , Note 8 ante.

16 Bilahari Kausikan, Note 14 ante.

17 Prashanth Parameswaran, Note 8 ante (2013).

18 Ernest Z Bower, 'China Reveals Its Hand on ASEAN in Phnom Penh', *Center for Strategic and International Studies*, http://csis.org/publication/china-reveals-its-hand-asean-phnom-penh; also, Donald K Emmerson, 'ASEAN stumbles in Phnom Penh', *East Asian Forum*. Retrieved on 1 May 2015, from http:// www.eastasiaforum.org/2012/07/23/asean-stumbles-in-phnom-penh-2/, (all accessed 01 May 2015).

19 Bagus BT Saragih, 'ASEAN's communiqué failure disappoints SBY', *The Jakarta Post*, http://www.thejakartapost.com/news/2012/07/16/asean-s-communiqu-failure-disappoints-sby.html; Ministry of Foreign Affairs, Singapore, 'Transcript of Minister for Foreign Affairs K Shanmugam's reply to Parliamentary Questions and Supplementary Questions, 13 August 2012', from Permanent Mission of the Republic of Singapore, ASEAN | Jakarta, http://www.mfa.gov.sg/content/mfa/overseasmission/asean/press_ statements_speeches/2012/201208/press_20120813.html, (all accessed 01 May 2015).

20 David Arase, 'China's Two Silk Roads: Implications for Southeast Asia', *ISEAS Perspectives*, Volume 2 , 22 January 2015.

21 'Disinvited', editorial in *The Philippine Star*, 5 September 2013, http://www. philstar.com/opinion/2013/09/05/1173771/editorial-disinvited, (accessed 29

April 2015).

22 Andrew Browne, 'China Bypasses Philippines in Its Proposed 'Maritime Silk Road'', *Wall Street Journal,* 10 November 2014, http://www.wsj.com/articles/china-bypasses-philippines-in-its-proposed-maritime-silk-road-1415636066, (accessed 26 April 2015).

23 See Shannon Tiezzi, 'The Maritime Silk Road Vs The String of Pearls', *The Diplomat,* http://thediplomat.com/2014/02/the-maritime-silk-road-vs-the-string-of-pearls/ , and; William Yale, 'China's Maritime Silk Road Gamble', *The Diplomat,* http://thediplomat.com/2015/04/chinas-maritime-silk-road-gamble/; Morgan Clemens, 'The Maritime Silk Road and the PLA: Part One', *China Brief,* Volume 15 Issue 6, http://www.jamestown.org/single/?tx_ttnews%5Btt_news%5D=43676&no_cache=1#.VXgLi2CJgdU, (all accessed 05 May 2015).

24 Author's interviews with regional scholars and diplomats, see; Irene Chan, 'China's Maritime Silk Road: The Politics of Routes', *RSIS Commentary,* No. 051, 12 March 2015.

25 Pasuk Phongpaichit, 'Financing Thaksinomics', unpublished article and part of a research project funded by the Thailand Research Fund under the Medhi Wijai at http://www.atimes.com/atimes/Southeast_Asia/ME20Ae01.html (no longer available); Awuso; C. Raja Mohan, 'Thai Transit', *Carnegie Endowment of International Peace,* Op-Ed 29 May 2013, http://carnegieendowment.org/2013/05/29/thai-transit ;; Royal Thai Embassy, 'Opening Statement by Her Excellency Ms. Yingluck Shinawatra, Prime Minister of the Kingdom of Thailand at the World Economic Forum on East Asia, http://www.thaiembassy.sg/announcements/opening-statement-by-her-excellency-ms-yingluck-shinawatra-prime-minister-of-the-kingd, (all accessed 03 May 2015).

26 'Thailand accuses US of meddling in its politics', *The Business Times,* 29 January 2015, http://www.businesstimes.com.sg/government-economy/thailand-accuses-us-of-meddling-in-its-politics; 'Thailand: A Pawn is moved in the US-China Great Game, *The Interpreter,* 10 February 2015; http://www.lowyinterpreter.org/post/2015/02/10/Thailand-pawn-moved-in-China-US-great-game.aspx?COLLCC=827513463&, (all accessed 03 May 2015).

27 'Council Discussed Loan Bill: Prime Minister Yingluck Thoroughly Explains Four-Part Strategy' [in Thai], *Post Today,* 28 March 2013, http://www.loc.gov/lawweb/servlet/lloc_news?disp3_l205403560_text; 'Bt 2-tn Loan Bill Rejected', *The Nation,* http://www.nationmultimedia.com/politics/Bt2-tn-loan-bill-rejected-30229085.html, (all accessed 05 May 2015).

28 'Thailand, China bolster military ties as US relations splinter, *The Bangkok Post*, http://www.bangkokpost.com/news/security/468332/thailand-china-bolster-military-ties-as-us-relations-splinter, (accessed 05 May 2015).

29 Pavin Chachavalpongpun. 'Thai General to solicit Japan', *The Japan Times*, 05 February 2015, http://www.japantimes.co.jp/opinion/2015/02/05/commentary/japan-commentary/thai-general-to-solicit-japan/#.VZIHLEaJhMt, (accessed 05 May 2015).

30 Mitsuru Obe, 'Japan Reaffirms Economic Ties With Thailand', *Wall Street Journal*, 09 February 2015, http://www.wsj.com/articles/japan-reaffirms-economic-ties-with-thailand-1423488868, (accessed 04 June 2015).

31 'Thailand, Japan sign bullet-train deal', *The Bangkok Post*, 27 May 2015 http://www.bangkokpost.com/news/transport/574655/thailand-japan-sign-bullet-train-deal; Masaaki Kameda, 'Abe announces $110 billion in aid for 'high-quality' infrastructure in Asia', *The Japan Times*, 22 May 2015, http://www.japantimes.co.jp/news/2015/05/22/business/abe-announces-110-billion-in-aid-for-high-quality-infrastructure-in-asia/#.VZILXUaJhMt, (accessed 04 June 2015).

32 'Sovereignty SCS: The new silk road on the sea and tensions in the South China Sea', *Nguyen Tan Dung*-Prime Minister's Website, 03 March 2015, http://nguyentandung.org/con-duong-to-lua-moi-tren-bien-va-cang-thang-tai-bien-dong.html, (accessed 03 June 2015).

33 'Petronas and Brunei Petroleum authorities sign agreements for mutual benefit', *Petronas Media Release*, 12 September 2013, http://www.petronas.com.my/media-relations/media-releases/Pages/article/PETRONAS-AND-BRUNEI-PETROLEUM-AUTHORITIES-.aspx; (accessed 04 June 2015).

34 Shahriman Lockman, "The 21st Century Maritime Silk Road and China-Malaysia Relations", *ISIS Focus*, May 2015; http://www.seatrade-maritime.com/news/asia/malaysia-onboard-for-chinas-maritime-silk-road-concept.html, accessed 04 June 2015; *Najib Bernama,*, 'Asean to hold more discussion on China's Maritime Silk Road Policy', 28 April 2015. The author thanks Mr Shahriman for sharing his firsthand experiences in China, and his valuable opinions and research findings.

35 Joint Statement by President Obama and Prime Minister Najib of Malaysia, 27 April 2014.

36 Justin Goldman, 'CARAT 2014: Advancing the US-Malaysia Partnership', *The Diplomat*, 25 June 2014, http://thediplomat.com/2014/06/carat-2014-advancing-the-us-malaysia-partnership/, accessed 04 June 2015. The author

thanks her colleague, Mr Collin Koh, for his valuable advice and knowledge on regional military issues.

37 Justin Goldman, 'Reaffirming the Marine Corps' Presence Mission', *Real Clear Defense*, 27 February 2015, http://www.realcleardefense.com/articles/2015/02/27/reaffirming_the_marine_corps_presence_mission.html, (accessed 04 June 2015).

38 Japan-Malaysia Joint Malaysia Joint Statement on Strategic Partnership Statement, 25 May 2015.

39 Rachel Chang, 'S'pore 'welcomes China's effort to systematically develop ties with Asean', *The Straits Times*, 12 September 2014.

40 Lynette Khoo, 'Singapore can leverage a revived Silk Road; PM Lee: Republic's role as transport, logistics, maritime hub could mean opportunities', *The Straits Times*, 11 November 2014.

41 Albert Wai, 'No clear ASEAN consensus yet' on South China Sea dispute', *Today*, 27 April 2015, http://www.todayonline.com/world/asia/no-clear-ASEAN-consensus-yet-South-China-Sea-dispute, accessed 04 June 2015; Ministry of Foreign Affairs, Singapore, *CNA: Momentum to resolve South China Sea disputes must not be lost: Shanmugam*, MFA Media Centre: Singapore Headlines, 03 April 2015.

42 Rachel Chang, 'Maritime silk road should keep disputes in perspective: Former foreign minister George Yeo', *The Straits Times*, 04 June 2015.

43 Zakir Hussain, 'Indonesia 'key in China's vision of Maritime Silk Road', *The Straits Times*, 04 November 2014).

44 http://www.brookings.edu/research/articles/2014/11/indonesia-maritime-liow-shekhar, (accessed 08 June 2015).

45 Vibhanshu Shekhar and Joseph Chinyong Liow, 'Indonesia as a Maritime Power: Jokowi's Vision, Strategies, and Obstacles Ahead, *The Jakarata Post*, http://www.thejakartapost.com/news/2014/11/13/jokowi-launches-maritime-doctrine-world.html; Darmansjah Djumala, 'Diplomacy for maritime fulcrum', *The Jakarata Post*, 13 December 2014, http://www.thejakartapost.com/news/2015/02/09/diplomacy-maritime-fulcrum.html; C.P.F. Luhulima, 'Superimposition of China's 'silk road' and Indonesia's maritime fulcrum', *The Jakarta Post*, 13 December 2014, http://www.thejakartapost.com/news/2014/12/13/superimposition-china-s-silk-road-and-indonesia-s-maritime-fulcrum.html; Shannon Tiezzi, 'Indonesia, China Seal 'Maritime Partnership', *The Diplomat*, 27 March 2015, http://thediplomat.

com/2015/03/indonesia-china-seal-maritime-partnership/, (all accessed 08 June 2015).

46 Zakir Hussain, Note 43 ante.

47 'China to Invest US$50 Billion in Indonesia's Infrastructure Projects', *Global Indonesian Voices*,   27 April 2015, http://www.globalindonesianvoices. com/20456/china-to-invest-us50-billion-in-indonesias-infrastructure-projects/; (accessed 02 June 2015).

48 Linda Yulisman, 'Indonesia to push China to realise investment', *Asia One Business*, 04 April 2015; http://business.asiaone.com/news/indonesia-push-china-realise-investment; Chris Brummitt, 'Desperate for Investment, Indonesia Plays China vs Japan', http://www.bloomberg.com/news/articles/2015-05-19/desperate-for-investment-indonesia-plays-china-vs-japan, (all accessed 10 June 2015).

The 21st Century Maritime Silk Road: The Beijing Consensus Revisited from a South Asian Perspective

5

Rana Divyank Chaudhary

Over the next few years, many of China's international economic initiatives are going to take shape in the form of urban development projects and supporting infrastructure for its foreign partners. For over a decade, China's leaders have voiced their aim to revive the past glory of the Chinese civilization. This is to be achieved by high rates of domestic economic growth, technological modernization, and connecting with the world's most vibrant and rapidly advancing economic zones. So far, Beijing's integration rhetoric has mainly hinged on the country's ancient cultural and trade linkages carried through the Central Asian and Southeast Asian corridors and the historical voyages made by Chinese seafaring explorers and religious pilgrims. Inherent to the vision that has been projected, is the memory of a pan-Asian order where China's periodic strength and prosperity translated into its pre-eminence in East Asia and a great degree of political sway over other states in the neighbouring regions.

Although today, the international relations of East Asia are driven by politics of insecurity and balancing as a response to China's increasing power, Chinese leaders stress upon the historically stabilizing influence of this power over Asia. As per this argument, China's desire would not be to upset the Asian or world order as it prevails today, but to shape it more favourably along the lines prevalent during the periods of relative peace when an imperial China was politically unified, economically open and stable, and culturally advanced. China would build upon this vision by fusing together national interest and global ambitions with active neighbourhood diplomacy and new economic partnerships. Its future projects seek to draw momentum from these shared narratives of world history, such as the ancient Silk Route. The Silk Road Economic Belt

(SREB) and the 21st Century Maritime Silk Road (二十一 世纪 海上 丝 绸 之路/ *èrshíyī shìjì hǎishàng sīchóu zhī lù*), together phrased as 'One Belt, One Road Initiative' (BRI), are believed to be the most significant steps taken by Beijing towards integrating the Chinese economy with other regions. In the BRI, China's current generation of leaders finally seem to have a blueprint of what their vision would contain and what it would offer to the world in material terms.

The aim of this chapter is to examine the Maritime Silk Road (MSR) from a South Asian perspective. The paper is divided into three structural segments. First, it briefly lays out the MSR's core elements in terms of its goals, nodes, funding, existing and planned infrastructure, and routes in this region. The second segment provides a projected assessment of the South Asian politico-economic space, which the MSR has to negotiate if it is to fulfil its goals. This segment draws on different South Asian perspectives originating in government, academic, strategic, and media sources to gain a sense of the responses developing in the region to China's expanding economic reach. The third and concluding segment analyzes the issue based on the conceptual framework of the 'Beijing Consensus'. This has been used as a Chinese model for economic relations/institutions to examine the factors underpinning Chinese interests in South Asia and evaluate the broad implications of the MSR for both China and South Asia.

The Roadmap for South Asia

China's efforts in the present seem concentrated on publicizing the BRI initiatives on high-profile multilateral forums and through a range of media and cultural activities.[1] Surely, this has served to appetize the international community, which is closely following these developments, and has got the attention necessary for the BRI to garner support among prospective partners. Finer details on the MSR's likely projects and concomitant fund allocation remain vague at this point with most sources dependent on Chinese official releases. The initiative is to consist of networks of railways, roads, oil and gas pipelines, power grids, internet networks, and maritime infrastructure to be developed in collaboration with partnering countries.[2] In South Asia, this would primarily link designated ports in the Northern Indian Ocean, which include Chinese-supported newly developed ports, and overland economic corridors on the Indian subcontinent.

Figure 1: Official Chinese media representation of the '21st Century Maritime Silk Road'

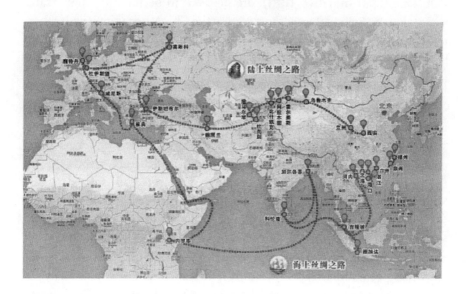

Source: xinhuanet.com

The China-Pakistan Economic Corridor and the Bangladesh-China-India-Myanmar (BCIM) Economic Corridor would connect the MSR with the SREB and bring all South Asian economies into the proposed network. The latest official maps show Kolkata (India) and Colombo (Sri Lanka) as designated nodal ports of the MSR. Other ports such as Hambantota (Sri Lanka), Ihavandhippolhu (Maldives), Gwadar (Pakistan), and Kyaukpyu (Myanmar) – all developed with Chinese support – are also likely to be part of the network although these have not been shown on the official maps yet (See Figure). This could be to avoid a repeat of the 'string of pearls' controversy before the MSR actually takes off. Some sources have also indicated Chittagong (Bangladesh) as a likely node for the MSR.[3]

The BRI initiative is financially supported by a dedicated fund of US$40 billion to be raised by Chinese-owned Silk Road Fund Co. Ltd. The company has reportedly begun to function with US$10 billion in the first phase, raised from the Chinese foreign exchange reserves and supporting state-owned companies, namely the China Investment Corp., Export-Import Bank of China, and the China Development Bank.[4] There are also reports of a Maritime Silk Road Bank (海上丝绸之路银行/*hǎishàng sīchóu zhī lù yínháng*) which would raise investments worth RMB100 billion.[5] The Silk Road Funds are also concurrent with the Asian Infrastructure Investment Bank (AIIB) and the BRICS New Development Bank, two other international financial institutions floated with China as a founding member and source of initial funding. Much of the MSR's facilitation would depend on the progress made by these associated institutions and on the expansion of bilateral trade ties and free trade agreements between China and South Asian countries.

In view of the BRI's nebulous status at present, it is also pertinent to examine the aspect of public diplomacy which has recently found great emphasis in Chinese foreign policy. China has distanced the BRI from comparisons with the post-War Marshall Plan by emphasizing its non-exclusive cooperative approach to the various regions and countries.[6] The BRI, and by extension the MSR, is supposed to be "synergized with existing regional cooperative mechanisms."[7] This fits with the regional sub-groupings besides the bilateral ties, which involve China as a stakeholder in South Asia. Chinese sources on the MSR have also stressed upon "equal-footed consultation" in the future development of the initiative. Thus far, the rhetoric has found welcoming audience amongst the smaller and lesser developed countries and so is the case in South Asia. The MSR, by design, gives the impression of an even-handed approach towards India, Sri Lanka, Bangladesh, Maldives, Pakistan, and Myanmar. The latest release from China's National Development and Reforms Commission, 'Vision and Actions on Jointly Building Silk Road Economic Belt and 21st-Century Maritime Silk Road' (推动共建丝绸之路经济带和21世纪海上丝绸之路的愿景与行动/*Tuīdòng gòng jiàn sīchóu zhī lù jīngjì dài hé 21 shìjì hǎishàng sīchóu zhī lù de yuànjǐng yǔ xíngdòng*) outlines the MSR's broad interest areas in the most comprehensive fashion.[8] But, the document's references to nearly every area of possible political and economic collaboration with other countries still makes it a difficult task to disaggregate the initiative's fundamental thrust areas. It is too early to ascertain how China would tackle hard economics as the MSR's top priority and how it will forge a lasting political consensus in South Asia where it is neither seen as neutral nor benign in equal measures by all the states.

Regional Perspectives

Expectedly, the South Asian perspectives on the MSR are both diverse as well as ambivalent. China is not only seen as a balancer against India in this region but also as an economic giant with tremendous one-sided advantages in terms of trade and commerce. For countries both large and small, this renders a narrower range of options when bargaining for self-interest with China. The MSR would bring new sets of challenges and opportunities to this milieu. New projects, trade agreements, and financial aid from China, would all gain more complexity with the MSR's ultimate goal of deepening sub-regional and inter-state trade links. But, far more obvious is this region's hunger for investment, infrastructure, and job/wealth-creation, all of which is envisaged by China's proposed mutual 'dream'. These imperatives form the basis of South Asia's responses to the MSR.

Pakistan

Pakistan has significant stakes in the BRI on account of two major Chinese-supported projects – the China-Pakistan Economic Corridor worth US$45 billion and the Gwadar port. It has long been seen as China's most reliable South Asian ally but their bilateral cooperation is steeped in unevenly-shared security interests and one-sided military aid. The Corridor is aimed at developing Pakistan's poor border regions and China's Xinjiang province. Prime Minister Nawaz Sharif highlighted Pakistan's interest in linking both Karachi and Gwadar ports with the proposed MSR at the 2014 Boao Forum.[9] The Chinese Ambassador to Pakistan, Sun Weidong has promised Chinese investments into Pakistan's power and energy sectors.[10] However, the underlying rationale for China-Pakistan relations are likely to remain security/strategic interests-driven. Both countries lend each other support and advocacy in fighting domestic ethno-nationalist movements and external strategic leverage – against both India and the US on grand political issues.[11] To these ends, Pakistan's support for the MSR would draw from the history and temper of Beijing-Islamabad relations and it would hope to draw the most comprehensive returns from the project. This is notwithstanding the known hurdles in Pakistan's domestic political and economic space which have adversely affected Chinese investments in the short and mid-term.[12]

Sri Lanka

Perspectives from Sri Lanka show a considerable degree of optimism regarding the island's inclusion in the MSR. China's position as the leading investor in the country and its financial backing for a number of port-development projects in Colombo, Hambantota, and Trincomalee are a part of making Sri Lanka the Indian Ocean hub for the MSR-related cargo and shipping.[13] Although the newly elected Sirisena government had suspended works on the Colombo Port City project, it seems to have resumed with the president's consent after he visited Beijing.[14] This has been taken as a confirmation of China's indispensability to the Sri Lankan economy, particularly when neighbouring India's investments are no match for the Chinese corporate construction behemoth. It is to be noted that Sirisena's campaign pledges to review all Chinese-backed projects did momentarily bring an active component of South Asian strategic power-play into focus. Chinese-built infrastructure on the island is too close for India's comfort.

India

In India, the MSR has led to an expanding discourse on which way to lean when it comes to the pursuit of national self-interest in Sino-Indian relations. Sharper manifestations of the MSR in the security realm may be debated for now but they are certainly on the horizon for many Indian analysts. New Delhi has aligned in favour of the AIIB, BRICS NDB, and the BCIM Economic Corridor but has reserved its decision to collaborate in the MSR pending the exact details of its plans. This too, is seen as originating from the China-threat outlook in the strategic community. However, a number of commentators have also argued in favour of taking a more self-assured standpoint and joining the MSR to explore opportunities and its full implications by being a part of it. These arguments refer to China's 16-character strategy for the Indian Ocean [meticulously choose points, develop a low-key layout, choose cooperation, and slowly permeate (精心选点,低调布局,合作为先,缓慢渗透/Jīngxīn xuǎn diǎn, dīdiào bùjú, hézuò wéi xiān, huǎnmàn shèntòu)] as indicative of Indian and Chinese ambitions inexorably intersecting in the future.[15] India is advised to join the BRI in a way that ensures the option to influence the initiative's developments and better secure India's interests. Further, the Indian chambers of commerce too agree that the prospective gains from economically collaborating with

China would bolster India's own capabilities regardless of how the MSR's politics shape up. [16]

The Beijing Consensus in South Asia

The MSR is both a masterstroke in China's symbolic diplomacy and an unprecedented economic outreach strategy. Chinese foreign policy seeks to go global and is keen on innovative strategies commensurate with its growing capabilities. China has also demonstrated the capability to follow rhetoric with implementation efforts. Without a doubt, this is to make up for the decades of self-imposed reticence in global affairs while the country underwent reforms and an arduous modernization phase. The unveiling of the MSR project by the Chinese leaders encapsulates this goal.

At its outset, the MSR seems ambitious in its geographic coverage and could be faulted for overlooking the myriad of geo-political constraints and region-specific hurdles in its way. But, building upon existing partnerships and the enhanced capabilities showcased by China's current set of leaders, the implementation of the project does not seem far-fetched. In this regard, the prism of the 'Beijing Consensus' (北京共识/*Běijīng gòngshì*) would be useful to plot the likely trajectory of the MSR as one of China's most high-profile strategic initiatives and its attendant consequences. Viewed from within the South Asian region, the MSR is a useful case to critically recast the concept of Beijing Consensus and expand its analytical reach.

Therefore, two key questions to be answered here are: (a) How are the concept's tenets relevant to a prognosis of the MSR's development in South Asia?; and (b) How do the changing emphases of Chinese foreign policy alter the 'Consensus' in Beijing's favour?

Revisiting the Model

In 2004, the 'Beijing Consensus' was coined to mark the increasing acceptability abroad of the attractive components of Chinese economy and its growth model.[17] It drew upon China's resounding success in indigenizing two crucial engines of rapid economic growth – enterprise and innovation. It was exemplified by industrial modernization and wealth generation on a gigantic scale without losing focus of absolute political stability and social order. The phenomenon signified that totalitarian political systems could still retain legitimacy in a globalized and purportedly uniform liberal world order by fusing economic pragmatism with centralized decision-making. Thereafter, its consequences have surfaced in China's external relationships and its manoeuvres in a unipolar international system.

Despite being non-conciliatory towards smaller and less capable neighbours on thorny issues, China places a high premium on economics in foreign policy towards the key regions of its interest. Coincident with China's growth story has been the notable receptivity of the developing economies of Africa, Latin America, and parts of Asia, to Beijing's economic overtures. Ostensibly, these states are trapped within the fault-lines that economic globalization and attendant wealth creation have failed to bridge. They also share several issues of intractability i.e., unstable polities and weak governance structures; lack of capabilities to attain economic self-reliance; internal security challenges and militarism; and authoritarian ruling elites in many cases. For them, engaging China has served as a way out of the Washington Consensus and its gatekeeping institutions (World Bank, IMF, etc.), which emphasize trade liberalization, deregulation, and decentralization. China epitomizes the Asian development model and the validity of pragmatism and autonomy for economies starting from a low level of development.

Although, it has been debated whether the 'Beijing Consensus' is accurate about Chinese economic exceptionalism, it certainly captures a quasi-Sinophilic turn and tendency in the Third World.[18] At a time when China's international profile is rising, this brings to fore two conclusive takeaways: (a) Due to its economic prowess, China now wields an asymmetric advantage vis-à-vis the United States and other great powers; and (b) China can bypass its external containment in world politics by employing this advantage in regions where states are characteristically susceptible to its influence and predisposed to favour it.[19]

Consequently, the Beijing Consensus is relevant to extrapolate issues of strategic consequences driven by the changing characteristics of Chinese foreign policy. Its predictive power continues to be in gauging China's regional and global outreach despite adverse perceptions, its own limited hard power, and the overarching primacy of the United States. The hype foreshadowing the 'One Belt and One Road' (一带一路/yī dài yī lù) initiative, its maritime element, and the Chinese efforts to actualize it, resonate with the model's core formulations.

The South Asian Context

The MSR (See Figure) holds significant ideological and political implications for South Asia. Much has been said about China's 'String of Pearls' which mapped the Beijing-supported port infrastructure projects in Myanmar, Sri Lanka, Pakistan, and so on. It is worth noting here that the Chinese projects have also faced resistance and delay in some cases.[20] The onset of political reforms in Myanmar since 2011 and improvement in relations with the West, and the recent political transition in Sri Lanka in 2015 suggest similar trends.[21][22] Yet, China engages in bilateral partnerships with all the South Asian littorals in varying capacities. Barring India, all of these states also have shared politico-economic and security vulnerabilities and a favourable disposition towards China's gradual advent into the regional maritime space. Further, China is also nodal to multilateral groupings such as the Bangladesh-China-India-Myanmar Forum for Regional Cooperation (BCIM). India is also tied to China by the Brazil-Russia-India-China-South Africa (BRICS) and its associated projects and funds.

In India's case, the MSR discourse is already reinforcing earlier narratives about the Chinese attempts of strategic encirclement to an extent.[23] The security dimensions of Chinese investments in South Asia constitute a sustained debate within the region. Moreover, it has caused fresh concerns in New Delhi about trailing behind its primary 'rival' besides missing an opportunity to foster economic connectivity in the developing world far beyond its shores. The Indian Prime Minister Narendra Modi has toured widely and pitched the idea of India taking greater responsibility for the prosperity and stability of the Indian Ocean Region (IOR).[24] In addition to endorsing the region's shared ethno-cultural heritage, he has reiterated India's sensitivity to the interests of smaller states in the region. This is a significantly proactive and inclusive consensus-building approach. Whether this would serve as a counter to China's economics-centric materialist initiative or be complementary to it would depend on India's future move with respect to the MSR. China has, indeed, mooted the concurrence of the two approaches and the scope for cooperation with India.[25]

Consensus, ultimately, requires the hallmark of voluntary acceptance. Fears of Chinese coercion and biased selectivity can undercut a nascent South Asian consensus. Conversely, achieving such acceptance in its most populous Asian neighbourhood, which is also nestled between both the

'Belt' and the 'Road' versions of the Silk Route, would give a great fillip to China's economic diplomacy. While parts of Europe too have shown willingness to collaborate in the landward 'Silk Road Economic Belt' (*sichou zhilu jingji dai*), obtaining India's cooperation for the MSR would be the high watermark of Chinese influence in South Asia and the IOR.

India's support for the initiatives, as already argued for in some quarters, would further enhance the Beijing Consensus's currency.[26] In addition, the endorsement of a high-value Chinese initiative by a liberal market economy would also dilute the Consensus's ideological hue. Furthermore, forging a South Asian consensus supplants China's responsibility with respect to international burden-sharing and highlights its constructive efforts for regional and global prosperity and stability. It counters accepted strategic wisdom that to balance against India, China draws other South Asian states away from New Delhi through its diplomacy, military support, and economic concessions. The MSR's progress would also downplay China's visible assertiveness in the disputes in East and Southeast Asia and serve as a decisive diplomatic counter to its detractors.

The conditions in South Asia and the Asian security environment augur positivity for the Chinese initiative despite known hurdles. The US's rebalancing towards Asia and China's troubles in East and Southeast Asia vividly contextualize Chinese interests in South Asia and the asymmetric potential of its economic leverage. In this respect, the introduction of a Chinese proposed-organized-funded-moderated trade and commerce network to the South Asian milieu appears intuitive and fits the puzzle espoused by the Beijing Consensus. Compared to the other regions, where China's contentious maritime interests and claims tend to create sharper divides, South Asia's geographic discontinuity and India's presence as a self-secure anchor would, in fact, give the MSR a counterweight and facilitate its soft landing. China's cooperative forays into South Asia have also elicited eager soft-balancing efforts from India. Hedging between the two giants by smaller states would keep the regional economic power play stable. Evidently, the MSR traverses overlapping spheres of inter-state relations in this region.

Recasting the Consensus

The Beijing Consensus is poised to enter South Asia albeit in an adaptive sense. The arguments given above present a case for recasting this model to make it more perceptive of the changing ideological and political elements of Chinese foreign policy. Firstly, it might no longer be relevant to pitch the model in terms of a specific typology of states aligning with China. China itself shifts away from the 'no-strings-attached' treatment towards its smaller partners in favour of greater material gains and political leverage. Secondly, unlike its present form, an adapted Consensus does not harbinger the definitive decline of existing alignments, international institutions, and regional orders owing to China's prominence. Instead, it captures the changing and new foundations of China's diplomatic agenda. A refashioned model would also provide with an outline of China's new external partnerships and support networks.

Interestingly, if the MSR takes shape, it will create channels for global influences to reach China's doorstep as well. Following the scholarly line of argument, which depicts China as a *status-quoist* power, enhanced connectivity with the world deepens Beijing's socialization within the international system. This leads to a benign decentring of 'Beijing' from the 'Consensus' even as the network of China's consenting partners grows bigger and more complex. Such an outcome certainly seems desirable from the Chinese perspective. The lion's share of China's relative gains is predicated on smoothening resistance and cultivating favourable perceptions abroad. The MSR constitutes China's thrust to achieve these ends by creating and coalescing parallel inter-state and regional networks within the present international order. On offer to China's new partners are greater equality of status and autonomy in collaboration. This significantly tempers the gatekeeping powers of prevailing institutions and of the states that currently enjoy dominance in them.

Notes and References

1   See 'Cultural' and 'Activities' sections on http://www.xinhuanet.com/english/special/silkroad/, (accessed 17 March 2015).

2   Lirios, Dino. "New Silk Road Trade To Top US$2.5 Trillion, Says Xi Jinping." *China Topix*, 30 March 2015 http://www.chinatopix.com/articles/44159/20150330/new-silk-road-trade-to-top-2-5-trillion-says-xi-jinping.htm#, (accessed 01 April 2015).

3   "One belt, one road." *The Economist Intelligence Unit*, 20 January 2015, China section http://country.eiu.com/article.aspx?articleid=1252682109&Country=China&topic=Economy, (accessed 18 March 2015).

4   "China's Silk Road Fund Starts Operation." *Xinhua*, 16 February 2015, China section http://news.xinhuanet.com/english/china/2015-02/16/c_134001196.htm (accessed 20 March 2015).

5   "金融加码支持一带一路:海上丝绸之路银行正筹建," Ministry of Finance of the People's Republic of China, 13 November 2014 http://www.mof.gov.cn/zhengwuxinxi/caijingshidian/zgzqb/201411/t20141113_1158211.html, (accessed 20 March 2015).

6   "Commentary: Chinese Marshall Plan analogy reveals ignorance, ulterior intentions." *Xinhua*, 11 March 2015, In-Depth section, http://news.xinhuanet.com/english/2015-03/11/c_134057346.htm (accessed 20 March 2015).

7   Ibid.

8   'Vision and Actions on Jointly Building Silk Road Economic Belt and 21st-Century Maritime Silk Road,' The National Development and Reforms Commission of the People's Republic of China website, 28 March 2015, http://en.ndrc.gov.cn/newsrelease/201503/t20150330_669367.html, (accessed 31 March 2015).

9   "'Instrument of prosperity': PM calls for unlocking Silk Road potential." *The Express Tribune*, 11 April 2014, http://tribune.com.pk/story/693865/boao-forum-nawaz-urges-for-the-revival-of-silk-road/, (accessed 18 March 2015). Also see, "Boao Forum: Nawaz urges for the revival of Silk Road." APP Story in *The Express Tribune*, 11 April 2014 http://tribune.com.pk/story/694119/instrument-of-prosperity-pm-calls-for-unlocking-silk-road-potential/ (accessed 18 March 2015).

10 Year of Friendship: 'China Helping Pakistan Overcome energy shortage'. *The Express Tribune*, 30 March 2015, http://tribune.com.pk/story/861049/year-of-

friendship-china-helping-pakistan-overcome-energy-shortage/, (accessed 01 April 2015).

11   Andrew Small, 'Sound Byte: Pak-China ties as close as Beijing wants them to be'. Interview with Hassan Belal Zaidi, *The Dawn*, 31 January 2015, http://www.dawn.com/news/1160547, (accessed 01 April 2015).

12   Ibid.

13   TK. Premadasa, "21st Century Maritime Silk Road." *Asian Tribune*, 16 October 2014 http://www.asiantribune.com/node/85658, (accessed 19 March 2015).

14   Keith Johnson, "China, Sri Lanka, and the Maritime Great Game." *Foreign Policy*, 12 February 2015, http://foreignpolicy.com/2015/02/12/china-sri-lanka-and-the-maritime-great-game-silk-road-xi-port/, (accessed 30 March 2015).

15   Saran, Shyam. "India must join China's Silk Route initiative." *The Hindustan Times*, 18 March 2015, Analysis section, http://www.hindustantimes.com/analysis/india-must-join-china-s-silk-route-initiative/article1-1327985.aspx, (accessed 20 March 2015). For the article mentioning China's 16-character Indian Ocean strategy, see Goldstein, Lyle J. "China's Biggest Fear: US-Indian Encirclement," *The National Interest*, 11 February 2015, http://nationalinterest.org/feature/chinas-biggest-fear-us-indian-encirclement-12225?page=2, (accessed 20 March 2015).

16   'Silk Road projects could benefit India: CII official.' *The Economic Times*, 28 March 2015, http://articles.economictimes.indiatimes.com/2015-03-28/news/60578817_1_indian-ocean-chinese-president-xi-jinping-infrastructure-development, (accessed 31 March 2015).

17   Joshua Cooper Ramo, *The Beijing Consensus* (2005), http://www.fpc.org.uk/fsblob/244.pdf, (accessed 18 March 2015).

18   Ibid, p. 35.

19   Ibid, p. 3.

20   Peter Lee, "China looks again at Gwadar and Pakistan." *Asia Times*, 12 June 2013, http://www.atimes.com/atimes/China/CHIN-01-120713.html, (accessed 18 March 2015). Also, Adam Pasick, "China's cancelled Burma railway is its latest derailment in Southeast Asia," *Quartz*, 25 July 2014, http://qz.com/240436/chinas-cancelled-burma-railway-is-its-latest-derailment-in-southeast-asia/, (accessed 18 March 2015).

21   Yun Sun. (2014). 'Myanmar in US-China Relations' Issue Brief No. 3 (June) http://www.stimson.org/images/uploads/myanmar_issue_brief_3.pdf,

(accessed 18 March 2005). Also, C.S. Kuppuswamy, (2013), Myanmar-China Relations – Post Myitsone Suspension. Paper No. 5380 (January 28) http://www.southasiaanalysis.org/node/1149, (accessed 18 March 2015).

22   Shehan Baranage, 'Will Chinese investors quit if Port City comes to a standstill?' *Lankaweb*, 21 March 2015, http://www.lankaweb.com/news/items/2015/03/21/will-chinese-investors-quit-if-port-city-comes-to-a-standstill/. Also, Sunimalee Dias, 'Sri Lanka will consider Chinese request to continue Port City work while probe continues', *The Sunday Times*, 22 March 2015, http://www.sundaytimes.lk/150322/business-times/sri-lanka-will-consider-chinese-request-to-continue-port-city-work-while-probe-continues-140486.html, (both accessed 23 March 2015).

23   Abhijit Singh, "China's Maritime Silk Route: Implications for India", *IDSA Comment*, 16 July 2014, http://www.idsa.in/idsacomments/ChinasMaritimeSilkRoute_AbhijitSingh_160714.html. Also, Arun Sehgal, "China's Proposed Maritime Silk Road (MSR): Impact on Indian Foreign and Security Policies", *Centre for China Analysis and Strategy*, July 2014, http://ccasindia.org/issue_policy.php?ipid=21,(both accessed 18 March 2015).

24   'Modi's Indian Ocean Tour.' *The Hindu*, 19 March 2015, http://www.thehindu.com/news/national/modis-indian-ocean-tour/article6982840.ece, (accessed 22 March 2015).

25   China says 'Mausam' can be linked to 'One Belt One Road', *Deccan Herald*, 05 March 2015, http://www.deccanherald.com/content/463755/china-says-mausam-can-linked.html, (accessed 18 March 2015).

26   Shyam Saran, Note 16. Also see, Gurpreet S Khurana, 'India's Approach to China's Maritime Silk Road: An Alternative View,' *National Maritime Foundation*, 17 Feb 2015, http://maritimeindia.org/CommentryView.aspx?NMFCID=8390, Vijay Sakhuja, "Maritime Silk Road: Can India Leverage It?" *Institute of Peace and Conflict Studies*, 01 September 2014, http://www.ipcs.org/article/military-and-defence/maritime-silk-road-can-india-leverage-it-4635.html, (accessed 18 March 2015).

China's Africa Push for MSR

6

Antara Ghosal Singh

The 'Vision and Action Plan on Jointly Building Silk Road Economic Belt and 21st-Century Maritime Silk Road', released on March 2015, by National Development and Reform Commission, Ministry of Foreign Affairs and Ministry of Commerce of the People's Republic of China, stated that "through this initiative, China, intends to connect Asian, European and African countries more closely and take mutually beneficial cooperation to a new high and in new forms"[1]. While connectivity between Asian and European countries has always been the cornerstone of China's flagship 'One Belt One Road initiative', however, 'Africa' figured for the first time, officially, in this strategic game plan[2].

It is in this context, questions arise 'Why Africa? Why now?' 'How will a blueprint for MSR in Africa possibly look like?' 'What is Africa's response to this development' and finally, 'What does it imply for India?' But, before we delve deep into these wide-ranging questions, it is important to explore the background of how the changing dynamics of China-Africa relationship has converged with the MSR narrative.

Changing Dynamics of China-Africa Ties and its convergence with MSR

China's engagement in Africa has a long history. Following the success of Asian-African Conference in Bandung, Indonesia, China began aiding African nations since 1955. Infrastructure development soon became the chosen area of cooperation. The Chinese funded Tanzania-Zambia Railway (TAZARA) constructed in the 70s became the epitome of China-Africa camaraderie. Today, China claims to have completed 1,046 projects in Africa, built 2,233 kms of railways and 3,530 kms of roads[3]. It is one of the most active players in the key sectors of the African economy such as aviation, highway, railway, telecommunications and power projects. The proposed 1,402 km coastal railway in Nigeria (China's single largest overseas project), the ongoing Mombasa-Nairobi railway in Kenya and the Addis Ababa-Djibouti rail projects in East Africa are some of the noteworthy Chinese investments in Africa[4]. Reportedly, 2,500 Chinese companies are operating in Africa today and creating over 100,000 jobs in the continent. China even claims that China-Africa cooperation has contributed to more than 20 percent of Africa's development.

Under the Xi-Li leadership, this relationship has been further fast-tracked. There have been back-to-back high-level exchanges between the two sides in recent years and newer, more innovative pledges taken, replacing the older and more conventional ways of interactions. For instance in 2014, after taking office, President Xi Jinping visited Africa (Tanzania, South Africa and Republic of Congo) as a part of his maiden overseas visits symbolising the continent's rising importance in Chinese foreign policy. Soon after Premier Li Keqiang undertook a four-country Africa tour visiting Ethiopia, Angola, Kenya, and Nigeria and 13 African leaders visited China during the year[5]. Again, beginning of 2015, Chinese Foreign Minister Wang Yi, as a part of his 'customary beginning-of-year Africa trip', visited five African nations - Kenya, Sudan, Cameroon, Equatorial Guinea and the Democratic Republic of Congo[6].

During these visits, the Chinese side initiated what they called 'China-Africa relation version 2' or China's new Africa policy based on 4-6-1 cooperative mode (ie. 4 principles like treating each other equally; consolidating solidarity and mutual trust among others - 6 key areas like industry, finance, poverty reduction, ecological protection, people-to-people exchanges, and peace and security and 1 model that is of FOCAC). While aiming to take the China-Africa trade volume to $400 billion by 2020 from $ 210 billion in 2013, the Chinese side is now focusing on developing a more holistic relationship with the continent by supplementing traditional assistance programs with more co-operation based programmes like social welfare, poverty reduction schemes, human development and cultural exchange. The idea is to shift its role from that of a traditional giver to a partner.

Although there was no official mention from either side during these visits about a possible link between MSR and Africa, however, it is only evident now that the groundwork for Africa's incorporation was on ever since. In fact, China's renewed focus on partnering African nations rather than being traditional assistance suppliers, its emphasis on economic cooperation, connectivity building, developing cultural contact, people-to-people exchanges, creating Africa talent pool etc. reflected the very essence and the core ideas presented in the 'On Belt, One Road' Vision Document.

Following these high level visits, Chinese scholars and strategists carried out a high pitch campaign in Chinese media highlighting the synergy between China's 'One Belt and One Road' initiative and Africa's own 'Development strategy in the 21st century'. They argued that it is time the two strategies should be combined to add new momentum to Sino-African ties and to further China's global interests.

Why Africa? Why now?

To better understand the reason behind this sudden Africa push for the MSR, it is important to contextualize the development against the backdrop of China's conventional Africa Policy. Contrary to the overwhelming perception that China's Africa policy is all about oil and gas, existing literature highlights that China pursues a multiple dimensional Africa policy directed at its multiple interests in the continent. For instance, in the realm of politics, the support of African countries is important to China in regard to its 'One China policy' and also on several domestic and international policy agendas at multilateral forums. In terms of economics, it provides enormous market opportunities to China in addition to vast reserve of natural resources. China also has security interests in the region. The presence of Chinese investments and personnel in the continent has increased manifold and ensuring their security is one of China's top priorities. In terms of ideology, China finds Africa as a fertile ground to export its development model and in terms of geopolitics, China feels that Africa is one place where it clearly enjoys an upper hand on the US and other European powers in terms of public perception and goodwill. These multiple interests, either exclusively or mutually, have influenced China's Africa policy from time to time. For example, from 1949-1979 political interests mostly dominated China's Africa policy – that is to garner Africa's support to avoid international isolation, to spread revolution in Africa, for solidarity on agendas like human rights, UN reform, Tibet, Xinjiang, Taiwan etc. From 1979-1990s when China started its reform and opening up; economics became the driving force of China-Africa ties. Under Jiang Zemin's 'Going out strategy', African resources and markets increasingly captured Chinese imagination. However, following the 2008 financial crisis, when Chinese exports to western markets started decreasing, Africa's importance further increased in China's policy circle.

In recent years, China's own economic transformation has become one of the key reasons behind China's coming up with global initiatives like 'One Road, One belt', or 'AIIB'. While adjusting to the new normal in the Chinese economy, China now has to chase new economic goals like creating new markets for Chinese goods, making resources available for its rising energy needs, moving up the global supply chain, cracking down on its polluting industries, keeping the business running for Chinese constructive companies and create jobs for its citizen. And, Africa offers a one-stop shop for all Chinese needs and objectives.

Chinese scholars argue that it is high-time China diversifies from investing its huge foreign exchange reserves in buying US government bonds to investing in infrastructure construction across the world. According to them, this policy will deliver higher returns and will also help address the large overcapacity in construction materials that it has developed at home.[7] And, when it comes to infrastructure construction, nowhere else in the world the need for infrastructure is so dire as in the developing world, especially in the African continent. Huang Jianhui, Deputy Director of the Center for Financial Research and Development, China Development Bank, writes in the China Daily, that no less than US$ 7.5 billion is required to be spent, on an average, on infrastructure in Africa each year, which is far beyond the $1 billion loan the World Bank has advanced in 2011 and this creates great opportunities for Chinese construction companies.[8]

Not just that, rise in labour costs in China, they argue, is weakening Chinese industry's comparative advantage and thus relocating its labour intensive industry to new places has become an utmost necessity. Chinese scholars argue that Africa, with a large number of surplus labourers, whose wages are a small fraction of their counterparts in China, is the right place for industry transfer on a large scale.[9]

Other than this, the latest developments around the MSR project can also be a trigger causing the Chinese to change the course of MSR and make it pass through the backyard of Africa. Although the initiative is projected to have received an overwhelming support from more than 50 countries[10] in the world, still it has always been at the centre of controversies and criticism.

First, the 'One belt, One Road' initiative, of which MSR is a part, has been criticised as 'China's Marshall Plan'[11] which is supposedly meant to serve China's larger ambition of becoming a dominant power and challenging the traditional ones. Second, there has been much negative publicity and criticism in the international media about the quality of Chinese investments abroad, especially after the MSR project along with other Chinese overseas investments have started running into trouble in certain partner countries like Sri Lanka, Greece, and earlier in Myanmar and Mexico.

Given the Chinese sensitivity towards its self-image and aversion to criticism, this negative publicity has not gone down well among the Chinese policy circle. The Chinese media is abuzz with articles accusing the Western countries in hyping up Chinese project failures,[12] the West being green eyed towards China's 'grand going-out' strategy and reiterating China's stand that the 'Belt and Road Initiatives' is no 'Marshall Plan' in substance and that China's gain is not at the loss of others.[13]

Interestingly, a section within the Chinese scholarly circle has been rather vocal about China's limited success in the realm of overseas investment. They note that China, in-spite of being the world's second-largest source of outbound direct investment, has more than half of its overseas investment projects which are non-profitable. They caution the government that 'blindly' pushing Chinese domestic enterprises to invest overseas under the Belt and Road Initiatives is unlikely to produce satisfactory results.'[14] An urgent need to incorporate pragmatism, perseverance[15] and prior local awareness[16] in China's overseas investment approaches is being strongly advocated by these scholars.

Under such circumstances, it is only likely that the Chinese leadership will be looking for more support and endorsement from newer sources in the international community for its flagship initiative of MSR. In this regard, Africa has been a time-tested source of steady allies for Beijing throughout history, supporting China repeatedly, both in the case of international and domestic crisis. Be it inclusion in the Security Council or the Tiananmen Square incident, or the One China Policy, African countries' support has always been crucial for the leaders in Beijing. In that perspective, it is not impossible that Beijing will be vying for African countries' support this time as well to add more credibility to the initiative and veer more domestic and international support and acceptance for the same.

In such a situation, it is not impossible that China will seek more support and encouragement for MSR from other sources. And, as history testifies Africa is one place which has always provided a steady source for allies and support to Beijing at different platforms at the time of its need.

How will Africa be incorporated in the MSR map - a possible blueprint?

The Vision and Action plan neither gives definite details about MSR's geographical spread, now is it aided by a pictorial representation or an official map. All it mentions is that the 21st-Century Maritime Silk Road is designed to run from China's coast to Europe through the South China Sea and the Indian Ocean in one route, and through the South China Sea to the South Pacific in the other. As a result, there are speculations abound regarding its exact layout and design, the real vision and mission, the mechanism of implementation and possible implications for the world.

However, based on the available literature, three possibilities look more likely. Some section of Beijing's official media uses a map (Fig. I) which indicates that the MSR will start from China's eastern coast, pass through Southeast Asia, the southernmost tip of India and East Africa, all the way to the Persian Gulf and the Red Sea[17]. It is actually a replica of the old Maritime Silk Road project dating back to 2,000 years ago. Ancient Chinese navigator from the Ming Dynasty (1368-1644) period, Zheng He, followed somewhat similar route and made his first contact with a coastal city in Africa, what is now Mombasa, in Kenya. Admiral Zhnag's *guanxi* with Africa, 600 years ago, is often propounded by the Chinese leadership to validate and enhance China's ties with Africa. Some Chinese scholars believe that the modern day Maritime Silk Road (MSR) will not be very different from admiral Zheng's Africa blueprint.

Figure 1: A Beijing Review map showing proposed reach of the New Maritime Silk Road

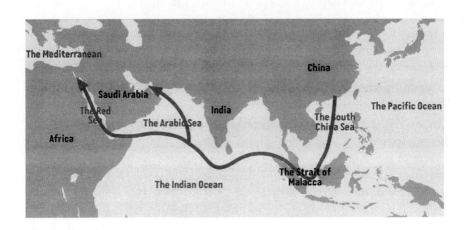

Source: *Beijing Review*

However, to some, in both Chinese and international strategic community, the above graphic is a much simpler version of a larger game plan by the Chinese side. They are projecting yet another version of MSR map, showing how Kenya and Djibouti will have a much bigger role to play in the modern Silk Road initiative. In addition, they say, China is funding and developing key ports in Tanzania, Nigeria, Mozambique, Madagascar and Seychelles[18]. However, it is not merely port development, but also local infrastructure development and connectivity within Africa, which is one of the top priorities of the Chinese in the continent. One Chinese scholar notes that while transporting a container in a cargo ship from Shanghai to Mombasa costs less than $ 500 US, transporting the same from Mombasa to Nairobi costs $1,500 US due to poor infrastructure[19]. So it is addressing this transportation challenge and connecting the vast hinterland of Africa to its Maritime Silk Road project that makes for China's long term plans in the African continent.

Figure 2   Map showing how Kenya, Djibouti will have a much greater role to play in the MSR initiative,

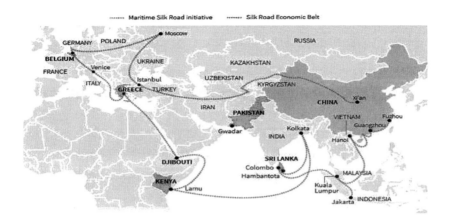

Source: *Reuters*

However, international commentators like Brian Eyler of IES Abroad, Kunming Center at Yunnan University, go a step further and endorse the view that China's MSR initiative is "all about Africa". In his article in the portal East by SouthEast, he argues that the main objective of the Silk Road is to support and facilitate trade between Asia and Africa, and not between Asia and Europe as was projected earlier. His argument is that trade between China-Europe has stagnated at $530 billion for last couple of years whereas China-Africa trade is on a constant rise and is about to cross $200 billion. China sees this as a great opportunity and is poised to capitalize on the same. But, it cannot operate the Maritime Silk Route, all the way to Africa, all by itself and thus needs others especially in South East Asia for port facilities and export goods, while itself sitting at the helm of the network, receiving the biggest share of income and resources from the set up[20]. In addition, China also wants to avoid the vulnerable Malacca Strait and is thus exploring an alternative route connecting its Yunnan province all the way to African coast through Myanmar, Thailand and Laos[21]. It has been reported that China and some other South East Asian countries including Thailand are already working together to develop 12 strategic ports which will receive and distribute cargo shipped along the Maritime Silk Road. Seven of these ports, reportedly, will be located on Africa's coastlines and these are Djibouti, Dares Salaam (Tanzania), Maputo (Mozambique), Libreville (Gabon), Tema (Ghana), Dakar (Senegal) and Bizerte (Tunisia)[22].

Figure 3 Map showing how seven key ports for MSR are located on Africa's coastlines

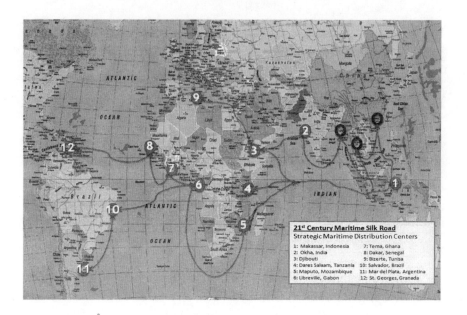

Source: *East by SouthEast*

Africa's Response to MSR

Before we explore Africa's response to MSR, it is important to understand Africa's response to China's growing presence in the continent in general. In spite of much criticism about China's large-scale involvement in the African continent, especially in the international press, the overall perception of Africa about China and Chinese engagement remain mostly positive, except for some countries like South Africa, Nigeria where the relationship lately has developed some degree of competition[23].

China being Africa's largest trading partner for five consecutive years and one of the key investors, most African governments attach great significance to China. However, it is not just African governments but people in general too (in many African countries) have a positive attitude towards China. Different researches conducted by international bodies like Pew Research and African counterparts like Afro-barometer show that most African people find Chinese engagement in Africa to be mutually beneficial. They say that favourable views of China outnumber critical judgements by two-to-one or more in most countries in Africa. About 85% of Nigerians, 77% of Senegalese, and 75% of Ghanaians view China as a national partner and have high regard for Chinese business acumen and science and technology.

However, in spite of such an upbeat setting, MSR is yet to find many takers in the continent, at least officially. Except for Egyptian President[24], not many countries have openly endorsed the MSR plan, while most are discussing the concept with their Chinese counterparts[25]. On the other hand, several African countries of late, has renewed their focus on development of blue economy as a vital part of Africa's future development and are coming up with their own maritime visions. South-African President Jacob Zuma recently set out his vision for exploiting the country's maritime resources, by launching 'Operation Phakisa' which aims at unlocking the economic potential of South Africa's Oceans[26]. Similarly, as the security situation off the east coast of Africa improves, the Seychelles government is supporting the development of a 'blue economy', using the Indian Ocean's resources for inclusive growth.[27] The African Union too expressed its commitment to embracing and developing the Blue Economy concept as a vital part of Africa's future development to be outlined in the AU's Agenda 2063[28].

African scholars are of the opinion that given Africa's limited maritime capacity in tackling both traditional and non-traditional security threats, it is important for Africa to build up partnerships with its neighbours and pool resources from other players, while at the same time voicing their concerns over militarisation of the Indian Ocean. On the economic front, they feel that the commercial aspects of the Chinese MSR could be integrated into Africa's own plan of developing its North–South terrestrial economic corridors and thereby strengthen the commercial attractiveness of the western Indian Ocean littorals of Africa. They are advocating that South Africa as the next chair of IORA, should take the lead to encourage non-African states to engage and align their Indian Ocean policies more readily with African positions and concerns[29].

What does it imply for India?

India shares a cultural, civilizational and historical linkage with Africa and therefore looks at a holistic relationship with the continent. According to High Level Committee on Indian Diaspora Report[30], 2000, of the 25 million strong Indian diaspora worldwide, around 3 million is distributed among different countries in Africa. Since independence, India has wanted to assume a leading role and responsibility in Africa as a major development and investment partner and security provider in the Indian Ocean.

According to a joint report by CII-WTO, India has been the fastest growing export market for African exports with growth of over 41.8% annually between 2005 and 2011 as against 28% recorded with China. On the other hand, India's exports to Africa has been growing at 23.1% between 2005 and 2011 – much comparable to the 25.6% exports growth achieved by Chinese exports to Africa. India- Africa overall trade grew at 32.4% during the period, which is higher than China-Africa trade growth at 27%. However, the total value of India-Africa trade (at US$ 63 billion in 2011) is only 38% of the value of China-Africa trade (at US$ 166 billion)[31].

Africa is a major supplier of natural resources for both China and India, mineral fuels account for 70% of Africa's exports to China, 80% of exports to India. Africa's imports from China and India are diversified, while China supplies for African demand for industrial machinery, electrical and electronic equipment, India's export basket to Africa have also undergone significant changes over the past decade as exports of cereals, food products and other low value-added exports have been replaced by refined petroleum, automobiles and pharmaceuticals that require substantial value addition.

Indian investments in Africa has increased manifold in the past decade in sectors like IT, telecommunication, automobile and energy. Researches indicate that it is likely to continue, given favourable conditions for investments and also, the Department of Industrial Policy and Promotion (DIPP), the investment promotion arm of the government, has identified Africa as one of the regions where Indian companies are encouraged to make investments.

Since outward investment data from both India and China to Africa remains largely sketchy, different researches provide different sets of data, however the general consensus is that both are important investors in the continent. For instance, according to IMF estimates, total Indian investments in Africa at the end of 2011 were US$ 14.1 billion – a share of 22.5% in total Indian outward FDI stock as against China's $14.7 billion by the end of 2011, or 2.6 percent of the total $570 billion FDI stock[32]. Another estimate puts cumulative Indian investments into Africa at over

US$ 35 billion (compared with more than USD 70 bn from China) and says India accounted for 5.8% of Africa's trade while China accounts for 16.13%.[33]

Not just trade and investment, India's role as a development assistance provider to Africa is expected to increase. India has already stepped up its assistance in Africa which has already seen an annualised growth of 20.5% between 2009-10 and 2011-12. Since, 1964, the cumulative figure for India's assistance to Africa is estimated to be US$ 1 billion. However, at the 2nd India-Africa Forum Summit in 2011, India pledged to extend LOCs worth US$ 5.4 billion to the continent until. (By the end of 2009, China had provided a total of 256.29 billion yuan. From 2010 to 2012, China appropriated in total 89.34 billion yuan of which Africa received 51.8 percent.) But, unlike China, where the majority of assistance goes into economic infrastructure (61 % by the end of 2009 and 44.8 per cent between 2010-2012)[34], Indian assistance is largely focused on project assistance, capacity building, institution building and scholarships.

India considers East Africa as its maritime strategic neighbourhood[35]. It has developed extensive strategic partnerships with several African nations, in forms of training cooperation and assistance, participation in the UN peacekeeping missions, defence cooperation agreements/MOUs, exchange of head of governments, defence ministers, secretaries, head of defence staff, military delegations, naval goodwill visits, assistance, joint exercises, defence equipment transfers and sourcing. India being one of the largest troop contributors at the UN, has played an important role in keeping peace in the continent. Indian navy has been at the forefront of the anti-piracy operations in the Gulf of Aden and along the coast of Somalia. Taking into consideration, the changing global security situation, India is looking at taking defence cooperation with African nations from just traditional security perspective to non-traditional ones involving conflicts, health, and terrorism among others.

In this scenario, it is apparent that China's increased involvement in Africa under the MSR banner will not only increase strategic competition for India in the continent but will also pose a threat to its security. Also, if MSR finds more and more takers in the region from South Asia all the way to Africa, India will be increasingly cornered and will be left with very little room for manoeuvre viz-a-viz Beijing on the MSR and on other pressing issues in Sino-Indian relationship.

However, delving deep into the China-Africa-India triangle, it is evident that interests and concerns of China and India actually converge in Africa and their roles compliment each other. Both the emerging economies are great advocates of South-South solidarity and are keen to prove the western proponents of Dependency Theory that dealing with natural resources do not necessarily mean neo-colonialism especially in today's time when the terms of trade are in favour of primary commodity exporters. Both want to prove the world that South-South cooperation can actually bring trade, investment, cause technology transfer and generate actual growth and development. At the operation level, both are concerned of regime instability, political violence, conflicts and other non-traditional security threats emanating from the region. While both are focusing on enhancing trade with the region, lack of infrastructure, trade facilitations and institutional frameworks are posing major roadblocks. Under such a scenario, the Chinese proposal of securing policy coordination, improving facilities connectivity, obtaining unimpeded trade, financial integration and people-to-people bonds[36] in the African continent under the MSR umbrella suits Indian interests too.

Furthermore, their involvement in the continent is also complimentary. As has been highlighted earlier, China's prime focus in the continent continues to be economic infrastructure building while India mainly focuses on capacity building, institution building and human resource development. This opens avenues for further cooperation between the two. As has been highlighted by CII-WTO joint report, India has already been exploring the idea of triangular co-operation arrangements in the continent in which it can utilize the comparative advantage or expertise of individual partner countries/multilateral institutions to maximise its contribution. One such trilateral cooperation programme has been U.S.- India - Africa Triangular Partnership Programme. The three-year programme was inaugurated in 2010 to improve agricultural productivity and innovation in African Countries like in Kenya, Liberia, and Malawi. Following the same pattern, India and China may also choose to work together in African continent under the banner of MSR or something else, with the ultimate objective of a win-win situation for all parties involved.

There are precedents where Chinese and Indian companies have been cooperating with each other in Africa. India's Oil and Natural Gas Corp. Ltd (ONGC) and China National Petroleum Corp. (CNPC) have not only carried out joint hydrocarbon exploration and production in Sudan but have also participated in joint bidding for energy assets overseas. India and China have also carried out coordinated patrolling and counter piracy efforts in the Aden sector and off the coast of East Africa. Recently they cooperated with each other while carrying out the Yemen evacuation drill. Officials from either side expressed hope that in future they would like to cooperate more in the humanitarian and compassionate ventures. There are talks of joint operations between the navies of both countries including the coast guards, air force and among the disaster management agencies. At the Seventh China-India Defense and Security Consultation consensus has been reached on strengthening cooperation in various areas, such as anti-terrorism exercises, personnel training, security of major events, combating transnational crime, food security and climate change.

Conclusions

As highlighted by the 'Vision and Action Plan on Jointly Building Silk Road Economic Belt and 21st-Century Maritime Silk Road', Africa is the latest entrant to the Maritime Silk Road Initiative. China's engagement in Africa has a long complex history but under Xi-Li leadership, the relationship has not only been intensified but have also been upgraded to what the Chinese side termed as 'version 2' and which can also be termed as a prelude to MSR's Africa tilt. The need for China's own economic transformation is at the root of this development. The growing criticism and controversy around the Chinese flagship project further acted as catalysts causing the Chinese to change the course of MSR and make it pass through the backyard of Africa. Since the vision plan does not provide details about the exact geographical extent of MSR, its exact layout and design, there are speculations abound regarding how Africa is going to be incorporated in the project. However, based on the available literature, three possibilities look more likely. Possibility I indicates that the MSR will start from China's eastern coast, pass through Southeast Asia, the southernmost tip of India and East Africa, all the way to the Persian Gulf and the Red Sea. Possibility II suggests Kenya and Djibouti will have a much bigger role to play in the modern Silk Road initiative together with Tanzania, Nigeria, Mozambique, Madagascar and Seychelles. Possibility III is that seven of the twelve proposed strategic ports along the MSR will be located on Africa's coastlines at Djibouti, Dares Salaam (Tanzania), Maputo (Mozambique), Libreville (Gabon), Tema (Ghana), Dakar (Senegal) and Bizerte (Tunisia). In spite of comparatively positive attitude towards China and Chinese investments in Africa, African countries have chosen to make a cautious/ measured response to China's MSR proposal. On the other hand, several African countries of late, has renewed their focus on development of blue economy as a vital part of Africa's future development and are coming up with their own maritime visions. Their objective is to encourage non-African states to engage and align their Indian Ocean policies more readily with African positions and concerns.

MSR's Africa tilt produces both challenges and opportunities for India. Challenge, because India has great stakes in Africa. Since independence India has always wanted to assume a leading role and responsibility in Africa as a major development and investment partner and security provider. Not just that, India considers East Africa as its maritime strategic neighbourhood. China's increased involvement in Africa under the MSR banner will not only increase competition for India in the continent but will pose a serious threat to its security. Also, if MSR finds more and more takers in the region from South Asia all the way to Africa, India will be increasingly cornered and will be left with very little room for manoeuvre viz-a-viz Beijing on MSR and on other pressing issues in Sino-Indian relationship.

However, the upside is that the interests and concerns of China and India converge in Africa. Their involvement in the continent is also complimentary. All these open avenues for cooperation than competition between the two. Now it is up-to New Delhi to weigh the situation, to do the cost benefit analysis before it decides to get on board of China' MSR proposal.

Notes and References

1   'Vision and Actions on Jointly Building Silk Road Economic Belt and 21st-Century Maritime Silk Road', *National Development and Reform Commission, Ministry of Foreign Affairs, Ministry of Commerce of the People's Republic of China*, 2015, (accessed 01 June 2015).

2   Chinese president Xi Jinping introduced the idea during his visit to Indonesia in October 2013. The earlier focus of the project was clearly on South East Asia. Chinese Premier Li Keqiang at the China- ASEAN Expo in 2013 emphasized the need to build the Maritime Silk Road oriented towards ASEAN. Foreign Minister Wang Yi, while speaking at the APEC Beijing summit 2014, further reiterated that the primary cooperation partners of the 'Belt and Road' initiatives are Asia-Pacific countries, and they will be the ones that will benefit the most. However, gradually the scope of the project got widened and different countries from South Asia, Asia Pacific and Europe have been incorporated in the programme. Now Africa is also included. Furthermore, the vision document says that the concept is now open for all willing countries in the world.

3   'The West's green eyes on China-Africa win-win cooperation', *China Daily (Xinhua)*, 31 January, 2015, http://www.chinadaily.com.cn/business/2015-01/31/content_19457842.htm, (accessed 12 March 2015).

4   Wang Xu, 'Sino-African ties look bright as trade heads toward $200b', *China Daily USA*, 26 December 2014, http://usa.chinadaily.com.cn/epaper/2014-12/26/content_19175501.htm, (accessed 12 March 2015).

5   Ibid.

6   'Chinese FM's Africa visit strengthens ties, cooperation', *Global Times (Xinhua)*, 18 January, 2015, http://globaltimes.cn/content/902488.shtml (accessed 11 March 2015).

7   Justin Yifu Lin, 'Industry transfer to Africa good for all', *China Daily*, 20 January 2015, http://www.chinadaily.com.cn/opinion/2015-01/20/content_19353077.htm (accessed 12 March 2015).

8   Huang Jianhui, 'A vision for financing Africa's infrastructure', *China Daily*, 06 February. 2015, http://africa.chinadaily.com.cn/weekly/2015-02/06/content_19507419.htm (accessed 12 March 2015).

9   Yun Sun, 'Africa in china's foreign policy', John L. Thornton China Center and Africa Growth Initiative, Brookings, April 2014, http://www.brookings.edu/~/media/research/files/papers/2014/04/africa-china-policy-sun/africa-

in-china-web_cmg7.pdf (accessed 11 March 2015).10   China's Silk Road strategy draws interest from over 50 countries: official, *Xinhua*, 25 January 2015, http://en.people.cn/n/2015/0125/c90883-8840754.html (accessed 13 March 2015).

11   Under the Marshall Plan, financial aid was offered by the US to the European and Asian nations to help rebuild their economies in the aftermath of World War II. It was largely aimed at containing the expansion of the Soviet Union and other communist countries.

12   'West hypes China's foreign project failures', *Global Times*, 04 February 2015, http://www.globaltimes.cn/content/905766.shtml (accessed 13 March 2015).

13   'Belt and Road Initiatives' no Marshall Plan of China, *China Daily*, 31 January 2015, http://www.chinadaily.com.cn/opinion/2015-01/31/content_19456082_2.htm, (accessed 13 March 2015).

14   Huang Yiping, 'Pragmatism can lead Silk Roads to success', *China Daily*, 25 February 2015, http://usa.chinadaily.com.cn/opinion/2015-02/25/content_19643172.htm, (accessed 13 March 2015).

15   Zhou Fangyin, 'One Belt, One Road' needs perseverance, *People's Daily* 03 February, 2015, http://en.people.cn/business/n/2015/0203/c90778-8844864.html, (accessed 13 March 2015).

16   Chris Dalby, 'Chinese SOEs need local awareness abroad', *Global Times*, 22 December 2014, http://www.globaltimes.cn/content/898118.shtml, (accessed 13 March 2015).

17   Yin Pumin, 'A second wind for an ancient route'. *Beijing Review*, Volume 58, No 6, February 5, 2015, http://www.bjreview.com.cn/Cover_Stories_Series_2015/the_maritime_silk_road.html, (accessed 12 March 2015).

18   Shannon Tiezzi, 'China's 'Maritime Silk Road': Don't Forget Africa', *The Diploma*, 29 January, 2015, http://thediplomat.com/2015/01/chinas-maritime-silk-road-dont-forget-africa/, (accessed 12 March 2015).

19   'Return of maritime Silk Road does not forget Africa', *China daily (Xinhua)*, 12 February 2015, http://www.chinadaily.com.cn/world/2015-02/12/content_19571496.htm (accessed 12 March 2015).

20   Brian Eyler, 'China's Maritime Silk Road is all about Africa', *East by South Eas*, 17 November 2014, http://www.eastbysoutheast.com/chinas-maritime-silk-road-africa/ (accessed 12 March 2015).

21   Atul Aneja, 'China steps up drive to integrate Africa with Maritime Silk Road'. *The Hindu*. 21 January 2015, http://www.thehindu.com/news/international/

world/china-steps-up-drive-to-integrate-africa-with-maritime-silk-road/article6802385.ece (accessed 21 January 2015).

22 Ibid.

23 Chris Alden and Yu-Shan Wu, 'South Africa-China Relations: Evolving Cooperation, Collaboration and Competition', 06 October 2014, *South africa institute of International Relations*, from http://www.saiia.org.za/opinion-analysis/south-africa-china-relations-evolving-cooperation-collaboration-and-competition (accessed 01 June 2015).

24 Wang Xue, Fouly, 'Egypt beefs up ties with China with landmark projects', *Xinhua*, http://news.xinhuanet.com/english/2015-06/04/c_134295140.htm (accessed 08 June 2015).

25 Hajira Amla, 'Mission to China: Seychelles Vice President Faure talks direct air links and Maritime Silk Road', *Seychelles News Agency*, 27 April 2015, http://www.seychellesnewsagency.com/articles/2827/Mission+to+China+Seychelles+Vice+President+Faure+talks+direct+air+links+and+Maritime+Silk+Road, (accessed 01 June 2015).

26 'Address by His Excellency President Jacob Zuma at the Operation Phakisa: Unlocking the Economic Potential of the Ocean Economy Open Day', *The Presidency, Republic of South Africa, Department: Planning, Monitoring and Evaluation*, 15 October 2014, http://www.operationphakisa.gov.za/Pages/Home.aspx, (accessed 01 June 2015).

27 'The Blue Economy: Seychelles' Vision for Sustainable Development in the Indian Ocean, *Chatham House*, 11 June, 2104, http://www.chathamhouse.org/event/blue-economy-seychelles%E2%80%99-vision-sustainable-development-indian-ocean, (accessed 01 June 2015).

28 'The Blue Economy: Key to Africa's Vision for the Future', Foreign Affairs Department, Ministry of Foreign Affairs and Transport, The Republic of Seychelles, 30 January, 2014, http://www.mfa.gov.sc/static.php?content_id=36&news_id=695 (accessed 01 June, 2015).

29 Chris Alden and Elizabeth Sidiropoulos , 'Silk, Cinnamon and cotton: Emerging Power strategies for the Indian Ocean and its Implication for Africa', *South African Institute of International Affairs, (Forthcoming)*, (accessed 01 June 2015).

30 http://indiandiaspora.nic.in/diasporapdf/part1-est.pdf.

31 'India-Africa: South-South, trade and Investment for Development', CII-WTO, 2013.

32   Xiaofang Shen, 'Private Chinese Investment in Africa: Myths and Realities', Policy Research Working Paper, *The World Bank*, January 2013.

33   Sarah Baynton-Glen, 'Africa-India trade and investment – Playing to strengths', Standard Chartered, 08 August 2012 from https://www.sc.com/en/resources/global-en/pdf/Research/Africa-India_trade_and_investment_Playing_to_strengths.pdf, (accessed 01 June 2015).

34   Information Office of the State Council, The People's Republic of China, 'China's Foreign Aid', July 2014, http://news.xinhuanet.com/english/china/2014-07/10/c_133474011.htm; Information Office of the State Council, The People's Republic of China, 'China's Foreign Aid', April 2011, http://news.xinhuanet.com/english2010/china/2011-04/21/c_13839683_5.htm   (both accessed 01 June 2015).

35   Ruchita Beri, *India Africa Security Engagement, India and Africa, Enhancing Mutual Engagement*, (New Delhi: Pentagon Press, 2014), pp. 115-130.

36   'Vision and Actions on Jointly Building Silk Road Economic Belt', Note 1.

7 | The Idea of a Maritime Silk Road: History of an Idea

Kwa Chong Guan

Chinese President Xi Jinping in his keynote address at the March 2015 Boao Forum[1] for Asia, provided details of China's vision for a new Silk Road Economic Belt and Maritime Silk Road, collectively labelled the "Belt and Road."[2] Xi first proposed a Maritime Silk Road during his visit to Indonesia in October 2013. The proposal for a Maritime Silk Road draws on historical images and metaphors of ancient sea lanes linking Chinese ports with other ports in the South China Sea and the Indian Ocean to envision China today participating in the development of a series of major ports on the Eurasian rim between China and the Mediterranean in order to promote maritime connectivity.

India in June 2014 launched a Project Mausam to revive forgotten memories of the Indian Ocean "world" as a "Transnational Mixed Route" along which not only rare and exotic commodities were shipped and traded, but also ideas and religions diffused, defining the boundaries of the Indian Ocean "world." India's Ministry of Culture has defined the project goals as reviving "lost linkages countries along the Indian Ocean shared with each other for millennia" and "creating links connecting discrete Cultural and Natural World heritage sites across this Indian Ocean 'world' via a "cross-cultural transnational narrative" to promote World Heritage.[3]

This paper reviews the history of this idea of a Maritime Silk Road linking China with the Mediterranean through the centuries which China is appropriating to frame its emerging foreign policy initiatives. This paper also reviews the assumptions underpinning India's Project Mausam's proposed documentation of the interactions between countries and communities across the Indian Ocean which continues to shape present-day national identities.

The Idea of *A Die Seidenstrasse*

It is to the German founder of modern geography as an academic discipline, Ferdinand Freiherr von Richthofen (1833-1905), that we owe the evocative term "die Seidenstrasse" to describe the myriad routes crossing Inner Asia linking Han China with the Roman West. Von Richthofen is best known for his multi-volume study of China's geography, which he approached from its inner Asian frontiers. From this perspective, not only the Chinese, but also the Roman and Byzantine and Indian empires were peripheral to the Eurasian Steppe, their historical development a consequence of the historical dynamics of the nomadic empires of the steppe. [4] Von Richthofen's interest was the history of Han Chinese and Imperial Roman geographical knowledge of the Eurasian Steppe. In von Richthofen's view, silk was the one commodity which linked Imperial Rome with Han China and explains their common interest in the geography of the Eurasian Steppe.

For von Richthofen, "die Seidenstrasse" referred to one very specific era of history, when Imperial Rome and Han China reached out to each other. "Die Seidenstrasse" according to von Richthofen, fell into disuse with the decline of Imperial Rome and the withdrawal of the Han from central Asia. The Tang did not so much revive the Silk Road as transformed it. Their Turkic origins led the Tang emperors to have a rather different geopolitical interest in their Inner Asian frontiers from that of the Han. Also, by then the technology of sericulture had by then been transferred or stolen to Byzantium and reduced Western demand for Silk. This shifted Byzantium and medieval European interest in the geography of Inner Asia. "The concept of the transcontinental Silk Roads...lost its meaning," von Richthofen wrote in 1877,[5] with the rise of an Islamic trading world.

Von Richthofen never ventured into Inner Asia. It was one of his students, the Swede, Sven Hedin (1865-1952), who was inspired to venture into Inner Asia. In a series of four perilous expeditions between 1893 and 1927 through Inner Asia, Hedin reached the Great Wall of China, identified the sources of the Brahmaputra, Indus and Sutlej Rivers and discovered the ruins of oasis trading cities and their Buddhist cave temples. He transformed his teacher's evocative, but narrowly interpreted metaphor of a Silk Road/s into a romantic vision for other explorers to lead long-range archaeological raids to strip the Buddhist cave sites of their paintings, sculptures and documents. Notable among them were Aurel Stein, Albert von Le Coq, Paul Pelliot, Kozui Otani and belatedly, Langdon

Warner, before the Chinese government closed the door to "foreign devils" stealing its treasures.[6]

Von Richthofen however recognized that the Roman West and Han China were also reaching out to each other across the Indian Ocean and South China Sea. But beyond the *Periplus Maris Erythraei,* a 66-paragraph *manual* of navigation and trade in the western half of the Indian Ocean compiled by an anonymous Graeco-Egyptian skipper and the later mathematical *Geographike Huphegesis* of the Alexandrine Greek astronomer Claudius Ptolemy, von Richthofen had little else to ground his attempt to understand Roman geographical knowledge of the maritime routes to China. He had even fewer Chinese sources to base any understanding of Chinese geographical knowledge of its South Seas. Von Richthofen concluded that as for the land routes, the sea routes across the Indian Ocean were pioneered by traders and mariners responding to an increasing wealthy Rome demand for silks and spices.

Constructing A Maritime Silk Road

It was to these fragmentary and ambiguous Graeco-Roman texts that the early 20th century European scholars studying the historical monuments of their colonies – Angkor and Champa in Indochina, Borobudur and its related monuments in the East Indies, and Sanci and other Buddhist cave sites in India– first turned to in their attempt to make sense of their history and their responsibility towards the preservation of these monuments under their charge. Confronted by the Indic iconography of the monuments they were attempting to restore, these European colonial scholar-officials turned to India, searching for the Indic precedents and provenance of this iconography and the process of its transfer across the Bay of Bengal. They inferred from the Graeco-Roman texts that it was a growing Roman demand for exotic and prestigious items of dress and consumption which drove Greek and Egyptian sailors and traders across the Indian Ocean in search of these items.

A generation of Sinologists, notable among them was Paul Pelliot combed the Chinese sources for their geographical knowledge of the "South Seas." Paul Pelliot (1878-1945), who lead the 1906 French expedition to follow the path of Hedin to Dun-huang, where he removed some of the more valuable manuscripts from Cave 17, reconstructed from the Chinese texts a lost emporium in the Mekong Delta which the Chinese knew as Funan. He also reconstructed the itineraries of two Tang envoys to the south and the Ming voyages to the Western Ocean.[7] The epigraphist George Coedès (1886-1969) collated the elliptical 7th – 8th century old Malay language inscriptions with fragmentary Chinese text references to *San – fo-qi* and Arabic textual references to a *Sribuza* to reconstruct a forgotten trading "kingdom of Sri Vijaya "up the Musi River in South Sumatra at Palembang today.[8]

The Chinese texts have since proved to be the most substantial and valuable corpus of evidence on the historical geography of the South Seas compared to the Indian or Arabic texts. These texts also indicate a limited Chinese awareness of the South China Sea and its trade through much of the first millennium current era. But the records of the second millennium indicate a growing Chinese awareness and engagement in maritime trade. It is these later record which appear to have shaped contemporary Chinese social memories of its active participation in the construction of a Maritime Silk Road.

Researches into the Chinese records combined with studies of the epigraphic and art history of the historical monuments by this pioneering generation of French and Dutch scholars[9] inspired and enabled a group of mainly Bengali historians to establish in 1926 a Greater India Society to "organize the study of Indian culture in Greater India" [I.e. Serindia, India Minor, Indo-China and Insulindia, as they defined it]. For these members of the Society, the overarching explanation for the presence of Indian culture in a Greater India was an Indian colonization of te lands the ancient Indians knew as *Suvarṇadvīpa or Suvaṇṇabhūmi,* the island or land of Gold. Trade in search of the land of Gold was the force that made a Greater India.[10]

However, the rise of the Mongols and Islam on the Indian subcontinent according to the pioneering European scholar, undermined the trade which had sustained the old Indianized states of Greater India. The Mongol expansion out of their steppe homeland precipitated a 13th century crisis in the peripheral empires of Inner Asia's frontiers. Mongol incursions into southwest China ended the Bagan Empire and facilitated Thai expansion down the valleys of the Menam to consolidate a new realm at Sukhothai, while an abortive Mongol expedition to Java enabled a new Majapahit realm to take over from Singhasari.

The members of the Greater India Society could well mourn the severing of these trade links and the loss of India's colonies in Further India. India's Project Mausam appears to be working towards a revival of these lost linkages with nations/countries along the Indian Ocean to "not only strengthen current ties between countries across the ocean, but also set a precedent for new bridges of co-operation and continued relations and interactions."[11]

Deconstructing A Maritime Silk Road

Post-World War II research by a new generation of scholars has revised this view of a Maritime Silk Road initiated by Roman demand for silk and other exotica, and that this Roman initiative qualitatively and quantitatively changed the nature of India-Southeast Asia relations. The classical Chinese texts have been more closely read for not only what they can inform us of the historical geography of the South Seas and its human geography, but also about how China administered foreign trade as offering of tribute to the emperor as part of the *heqin* system of "harmonious relationship" that assumes the superiority of the Chinese emperor and the inferiority of the ruler offering "tribute." The texts have also been read for what they tell of China's active participation in maritime trade from the time of the Song.

Field archaeology surveys and excavations have confirmed the existence of early maritime polities mentioned in the Chinese and other texts. More significant, excavations into the prehistory of the region have reconstructed a series of interlinked Austronesian trading networks connecting Southern China with Southeast Asia and India, enabling the later construction of a Maritime Silk Road. Excavation of an increasing number of shipwrecks in the South China Sea and the Java Sea since the 1980's is fundamentally changing our understanding of the nature and structure of trade and the ships this trade was conveyed on in the *Nan hai*.[12]

The Arab shippers and traders who had ventured into the Indian Ocean from the Gulf ports of Basra and Saifra along routes pioneered by earlier Persian and Jewish traders to Sri Lanka and across the Bay of Bengal to Śrīvijaya before heading north to Guangzhou, did not, as the pre-World War II scholars constructed, undermine Indian trade with its colonies in the *Suvarṇadvīpa*. Rather, Islam from the 7th to the 17th century inspired a world system which brought all the classical civilisations - Greco-Roman, Sassanid-Sernitic, Sanskritic and Chinese – into new relationships with each other. A new Indo-Islamic world *al-bahr al hindi* emerged in the Indian Ocean, drawing the Indian subcontinent and Southeast Asia tighter together to the Islamic core region of West Asia.[13] It may not be a coincidence that Borobudur, Angkor and the Ananda were all constructed during this era of *al-bahr al hindi*.

Research into the early modern maritime trade and trading diasporas across the Indian Ocean[14] and the South China Sea shows that Vasco da Gama's arrival at Calicut on 27 May 1498 was not the start, as K. M. Panikkar argued, of a quincentenary of Western dominance of Asia through control of the sea and truncated India's and China's trading relations with the rest of Asia.[15] The merchant empires of Europe largely competed for control of Asian trade with Europe. It was a rivalry which frequently escalated into conflict which continued into the 19th century colonial conquest for empire. But the intra-Asian trade of the Indian Ocean and the South China Sea continued unaffected by European rivalry, and enjoyed booms with increasing amounts of European money paid for Asian products taken to Europe.

Sixty years of research into the maritime trade of the South China Sea and the Indian Ocean has qualified and challenged the research of the preceding forty years represented in the researches of the Greater India Society. But by 1959 these revisions deconstructed and rendered untenable much that the Greater India Society advocated and lead the Society to disband itself. A new reconstruction of the connected histories of the South China Sea and the Indian Ocean is in the making.

The Maritime Silk Road Reconstructed

The emerging reconstruction of a Maritime Silk Road goes beyond von Richthofen's strictures on understanding "die Seidenstrasse" to refer to only sea shipping between Roman and China to an understanding of maritime links between the Persian Gulf/Red Sea and the Indian Ocean and South China Sea within the long cycles and connected histories of regions. The South China Sea and the Indian Ocean are spaces of circulation and networks along which peoples and goods moved and ideas and technologies seeped. The challenge to reconstructing a linear trajectory for a Maritime Silk Road, which starts with prehistoric Austronsian migrations out of Southern China, culminating with India looking East and China looking west again, is to also include cyclic trajectories of economic and trade history of the South China Sea and the Indian Ocean.[16]

The Graeco-Roman traders sailing to India and Han Chinese envoys pushing south to discover new worlds was arguable the incipient cycle of trade marking the beginning of a Maritime Silk Road. As on the overland road, where the oasis cities of central Asia and their Buddhist cave monasteries, especially at Dun Huang, is evidence of a close and complex relationship between commerce and Buddhism, likewise in island Southeast Asia, Buddhism had a close and complex relationship with trade across the Bay of Bengal. The creation of a Pan-Asian Buddhist World from the 4th – 8th century CE was another cycle of trade on the Maritime Silk road.

Concurrent with this cycle of maritime trade on the Indian Ocean was another cycle driven by Arab and Persian traders to construct an Indo-Islamic trading world. This Indo-Islamic world stretched in time from its beginnings in the Abbasids to end with the Safavids, Mughals and the Ottomans, and in space from al-Andalus to Quanzhou and the Swahili coast. There were, within this millennium long linear history of an Indo-Islamic trading world, a number of cyclic trajectories on the maritime routes.

The Portuguese capture of Melaka in 1511 did not so much disrupt Asian trade as to redistribute it to other ports. Portuguese demand for spices and aromatics, combined with that of the Dutch from the beginning of the 17th century, created a century long economic boom in Southeast Asia. The 18th century is a turning point in our reconstruction of a Maritime Silk Road and Indian Ocean "world." Up to that point of time, none of the Asian trading communities and their guilds perceived the need to occupy ports and control sea lanes. The sea was a great void crossed at great risks.

The Portuguese attempt to establish an *Estado da Índia,* a "state of India" based on armed shipping; control of a chain of fortresses and trading posts in the Indian Ocean to control trade through enforcement of a *cartaz* (safe conduct) system was therefore unprecedented.[17] The north Atlantic merchant adventurers and their trading companies however also followed the Portuguese in establishing a series of forts on the Coromandel and Malabar coasts of India and in island Southeast Asia. The conquest and occupation of territories, once initiated, developed a momentum of its own, and by the 18th century, these north Atlantic trading companies were transformed into rival merchant empires competing for control of the seas and its sea lanes. Their interventions and inroads into the hinterlands of their ports became the basis of European colonial empires in the 19th century. The challenge for Asian polities was to develop new strategies to respond and adapt to the creeping advance of the European colonial states. The culmination of their response to the dominance of the colonial states was a 20th century anti-colonial struggle for independence.

Conclusion

A substantial corpus of knowledge[18] was therefore available to UNESCO when in 1988 it launched a ten-year project entitled "Integral Study of the Silk Roads: Roads of Dialogue" to "highlight the complex cultural interactions arising from the encounters between East and West and helping to shape the rich common heritage of the Eurasian peoples." The focus of the Project was more on the overland roads which four Expeditions traced, and en route, convened 26 seminars. Only one expedition traced the maritime route in October 1990 voyage from Venice to Osaka.[19]

Nevertheless, as von Richthofen recognized, in the long cycles of history, the maritime routes are probably more significant than the overland roads. As the founding director (1902-5) of the Institut für Meereskunde (Institute for the Study of the Sea) in Berlin he should be aware of the significance of maritime trade and traffic. Almost a century and a half after Richthofen delivered his lectures on the sea shipping to and from China to the German Geological Society,[20] we have the evidence of trade, travel and transfer of technologies and ideologies linking China with India and the Persian Gulf and Mediterranean worlds.

The linear (and monolithic) narrative of a Maritime Silk Road reconstructed in the preceding paragraphs is about the connections and interactions of three different trading worlds loosely connected to form a "Maritime Silk Road" or Indian Ocean "world." They are a South China Sea trading world structured around tribute trade imposed by China; an "Indianized" world linking ports and kingdoms across the Bay of Bengal; and an Arabian Sea core of an Indo-Islamic trading world. New data from field archaeology and maritime archaeology, and new close readings of the classical texts are continuing to revise our reconstruction of a Maritime Silk Road and Indian Ocean "word" as more decentred and connected that assumed in today's interpretations of these historical metaphors and images.

Southeast Asia, especially the Malay peninsula and its Straits of Melaka, was not only the funnel through which West and South Asian aromatics and other luxury things flowed to China and Chinese silks and porcelains flowed across the Bay of Bengal to the Persian Gulf. The Malay peninsula was the crossroads of the Maritime Silk Road and its Melaka Straits ports were not so much entrepôts through which commodities were transhipped, but more emporiums, controlling the flow of commodities between the South China Sea and the Bay of Bengal trading networks. The Straits of Melaka was also a knowledge corridor along which the theologies of Asia's religions flowed. As the crossroads of the Maritime Silk Road, Southeast Asia drew upon, transformed and reworked the flows and seepage of peoples, ideas and things from China, India, West Asia and Europe. It is a role the Association of Southeast Asian Nations hopes to reassert itself as India Looks East and China Looks West with its proposals for a new Silk Road.

The narrative emerging from this reconstruction of a Maritime Silk Road is that the 18th century was a turning point, when Europe "diverged" from Asia and moved to dominate the Maritime Silk Road. Different explanations for this divergence[21] are leading to rather different understandings of the future of the Maritime Silk Road. Are we witnessing a new cycle of a Guangdong and Amoy reaching across the South China Sea and into the Indian Ocean to renew old trade links?[22] Or, are we observing the emergence of a new understanding of the South China Sea and Indian Ocean as part of a Global Commons for a more sustainable future?

Notes and References

1   The Boao Forum is a nongovernmental and nonprofit international organization proposed in 1998 by former Philippines President Fidel V. Ramos, former Australian Prime Minister Bob Hawke and former Japanese Prime Minister Morihiro Hosokawa. The Forum was formally inaugurated on 27 Feb 2001 at Boao in Hainan Province, where it continues to meet annually.

2   China's National Development and Reform Commission, in conjunction with the Chinese Foreign Affairs Ministry and Commerce Ministry has issued an action plan, an English translation, "Vision and Actions on Jointly Building Silk Road Economic Belt and 21st Century Maritime Silk Road" available at http://news.xinhuanet.com/english/china/2015-03/28/c_134105858.htm.

3   The Indira Gandhi National Centre for the Arts has been designated the nodal coordinating agency for the project, see http://www.indiaculture.nic.in/project-mausam.

4   Daniel C. Waugh, "Richthofen's "Silk Roads": Towards the Archaeology of a Concept." *The Silk Road* 5/I (Summer 2007), http://www.silkroadfoundation.org/toc/newsletter.html. See, C. I. Beck, *Empires of the Silk Road; A history of Central Eurasia from the Bronze Age to the Present* (Princeton: University Press: 2009) and, earlier; Owen Lattimor's classic, *Inner Asian Frontiers of China* (New York: American Geographical Society, 1940, repr. 1951 and 1962) for an Inner Asian approach to history.

5   Quoted in Waugh, Note 4 p. 5.

6   Peter Hopkirk, *Foreign Devils on the Silk Road; The search for the lost treasures of central Asia* (London: John Murray, 1980) for the story of the long-range archaeological raids led by Stein, Pelliot and others, which incurred the undying wrath of the Chinese, up to today.

7   Pelliot, "Le Fou-nan." *B.École franc. Extr.-Or* 3(1903), pp. 248-330; "Deux itineraries de Chine en Inde à la fin du VIIIᵉ siècle," *idem* 4 (1904), pp. 131-413 and, "Les grands voyages maritimes chinois au débute du XVᵉ siècle" *T'oung Pao* 30 (1933), pp. 237-452, continued in "Notes additionalles sur Tcheng Houo et survoyages," *idem* 31 (1935) pp. 274-314.

8   Coedès, "Le royaume de Çrivijaya," *B. École franc. Edtr.-Or.* 18 (1918), pp. 1-36.

9   Coedès in his benchmark synthesis *Les états Hindouisés d'Indochine et d'Indonesia* (Paris: Edn. E de Boccard, 1964) , the first edition of which was published in 1944, on the eve of Coedès' retirement as Director of the EFEO

in 1947, is still the definitive summary of the first 40 years of scholarship on early Southeast Asia.

10 Kwa Chong-Guan, (Ed.), *Early Southeast Asia viewed from India; An anthology of articles from the* Journal of the Greater India Society (New Delhi: Manohar Publishers for Nalanda-Sriwijaya Centre, 2013), pp. xv-xlvii for an assessment of the contribution of the Greater India Society to historiography.

11 Ministry of Culture, Government of India, *Mausam/Mawsim: Maritime routes and cultural landsapes; Concept Note"* at http://www.indiaculture.nic. in/project-mausam.

12 See Kwa Chong Guan, Locating Singapore on the Maritime Silk Road: Evidence from Maritime Archaeology, ninth to early nineteenth centuries, *Nalanda-Sriwijaya Centre,* Working Paper Series No. 10, Jan 2012, http://nsc. iseas.edu.sg/documents/working_papers/nscwps010.pdf

13 Richard M. Eaton, "Islamic history as Global history," in M. Adas, (Ed.), *Islamic & European expansion; The forging of a global order* (Philadelphia: Temple University,1993), pp. 1-36 on the centrality of Islamic history in global history.

14 See Om Prakash, (Ed.), *The trading world of the Indian Ocean, 1500-1800, History of Science, Philosophy and Culture in Indian Civilization, vol. III, part 7* (Delhi: Pearson Centre for Studies in Civilizations, 2012) reflects this shift in historiographical focus from an India turning inwards from the 16th century to an India actively responding to regional and wider global changes in the Indian Ocean. Also K. N. Chaudhuri, *Trade and civilization in the Indian Ocean: An economic history from the rise of Islam to 1750* (Cambridge: University Press, 1985) for a long cycle history of the continuity of Indian Ocean trade.

15 KM Panikkar, *Asia and Western Dominance: A survey of the Vasco da Gama epoch of Asian history 1948-1945* (London: Allen & Unwin, 1953, repr. 1959).

16 See Peter Coclanis, *Time's arrow; Time's cycle; globalization in Southeast Asia over la longue durée* (Singapore: Institute of Southeast Asian Studies / Raffles Lecture series 2, 2006) for an attempt to frame historical developments in Southeast Asia within these two metaphors of time.

17 The Portuguese (and Spanish) venture to control shipping and trade was arguably an attempt to extend their understanding of the Mediterranean as a closed sea over which Rome claimed jurisdiction or *imperium* . However, Roman *imperium* over the seas did not , as Hugo Grotius has argued, amount to a claim to *dominium* or ownership of the seas, which Grotius charged, the

Portuguese were attempting in excluding the Dutch from the trade of the Indian Ocean, on which, see Peter Borschberg, *Hugo Grotius, the Portuguese and Free Trade in the East Indies* (Singapore: NUS Press, 2011), pp. 78-105.

18 Highlighted in Vadime Elisseeff, ed., *The Silk Road; Highways of culture and commerce* (New York: Bertghahan Books, 2000).

19 UNESCO's programme statement and summary of the achievements of this project are available at *nesdoc.unesco.org/images/0015/001591/159189E.pdf.*

20 Richtofen, "überden Seeverkehr nach und vonChina im altertum und mittelaiter." *Verhandlungen der Gesellaschaft für Erdkunder zu Berlin,* 1876: 86-97, cited in Waugh, Note 4 above, p. 3.

21 See Kenneth Pomeranz, *The Great Divergence; China, Europe, and the making of the modern world economy* (Princeton: Princeton University Press, 2000) and J.-L. Rosenthal and R B Wong, *Before and beyond divergence; The politics of economic change in China and Europe* (Harvard: Harvard University Press, 2011) for the implications of different explanations for this "Great Divergence."

22 The argument for a 21st Century "Chinese Mediterranean" in the *longue durée* is made by François Gipouloux, *La Meditérranée asiatique: Ville portuaires en réseaux marchands en Chine, au Japon et en Asie du Saud-est, XVI-XXI siècle* (Paris: CNRS Editions, 2009). See also Wang Gungwu's insights into this analogy of "the Two-Ocean Mediterranean" in Ooi Kee Beng, *The Eurasian Core and its edges; Dialogues with Wang Gungwu on the History of the World* (Singapore: Institute of Southeast Asian Studies, 2015), pp.57-93.

	Revisiting Maritime Past: MSR and
8	**Project Mausam**

Adwita Rai

The new leadership in India and China have taken policy initiatives to redefine their position in the current global scenario. One similar aspiration both countries share is the growing interest in the maritime domain. China with its 'Maritime Silk Road' (MSR) has proposed to revive the ancient Silk Road 'through modern perspectives' while India has endeavoured to 'string together ancient cultural routes and maritime linkages to different parts of the world' through its 'Project Mausam'. The Chinese ambassador Le Yucheng spoke about the possibility of India-China cooperation linking MSR to India's Project Mausam, as both have similar foundations.[1] Apart from the fact that both are the outcome of Asia's resurgence, both concepts use historical assertions to substantiate their presence in the oceanic exchange network. This has generated multitude of inquiry to compare the parallel interests, analysing its geo-strategic, political and economic underpinning.

Since, both the concepts from the inception onwards, aim at 'reviving' and 'acknowledging' maritime past. However, despite the fact that both 'MSR' and 'Mausam' inherit claims through history, not much has been emphasized about their significance in re-shaping maritime history.

Maritime Discourse and Changing Historiography

Maritime discourse about the past has often been dominated by western centric typologies. The initial attention to acknowledge maritime engagements of historical significance was a European construct to exemplify their dominance and supremacy through the oceans. While, recording activities 'at sea' was a common phenomenon and can be dated back to the first millennium B.C., the need to exemplify the importance of 'matters maritime' began in the late eighteenth century. At this stage, European narratives started emphasizing their hegemony on the seas linking the 'Rise of the West' to their oceanic superiority. The basic impetus of these writings was the influence and affluence of the Imperial powers in establishing and exerting maritime networks. The writings were mainly concerned about how European colonization was not just a symbol of technological superiority rather a representation of its structural dominance in the maritime transcontinental network. The rise of industrial capitalism coupled with technological improvements like steam, shellfire, and armor facilitated European powers to play a decisive role. The overseas exchange network witnessed a radical shift as it led to the opening of new ports. This opening of new ports not just led to increase in trade exchange rather it also led to unprecedented spread of ideas.

Since the inception, overseas networks have been viewed through the prism of trade and economy. Time and again, scholars have equated maritime networks as trading networks and reconstructed maritime linkages to explore trade relations. The nineteenth century witnessed a gradual shift in academic writings as with the rise of nationalism among the colonies indigenous scholars started questioning the hegemonic apparatus. This initiated nations 'to define and identify their roles in exchange networks resulting in redefinition and new characterization of the overseas networks. Further, with the beginning twentieth century, when the nationalist movements started gaining momentum, native historians began to look away from the conventional understanding and began to delineating trade and its importance within the society. This drove nationalist historians to look beyond trade and economy and the scholarly writings gravitated towards the spread of religions (Christianity, Islam and Buddhism), ideas, culture and literary thoughts over the sea.

Despite a gradual shift in the thematic framework, not much has been explored about the shared past as the focus remains on trading networks. Also, the depiction of the maritime past has largely been constricted by marked boundaries of nations. The apprehension through which maritime past has been viewed has by and large left the participants out in the cold.

The recent initiatives taken by India and China have brought maritime past again into the limelight and attempts to question the perceived notion. Both, 'MSR' and 'Mausam' have reopened the historical interpretations and have shifted the focus of inquiry to 'many aspects of exchange networks.'

Maritime Silk Road and Chinese initiative

The concept of reviving ancient Maritime Silk Route to build 21st century Maritime Silk Road (MSR) was first proposed by Chinese President Xi Jinping, in the Indonesian parliament during the 10th ASEAN-China summit in 2013 to improve connectivity between China and Southeast Asian countries. Highlighting the essence of reviving ancient Silk Route Chinese president Xi Jinping said, it will build an economic belt along the Silk Road and Maritime Silk Road that will mutually benefit the participants.

The terminology 'Silk Road' has often been emphasized time and again in Chinese development strategy, be it 'Silk Road Economic Belt' or '21st century Maritime Silk Road'. The major impetus of recalling past for Chinese remains the Silk Road, as they view it as "the world's oldest, and historically most important route".[2] The term Silk Road is collectively used to explain the ancient trade network, which included both overseas as well as overland routes linking China to Central Asia,[3] facilitating human movements, exchange of goods, ideas and skills.

However, it is ironical that there is no mention of the term 'Silk Road' in any ancient sources. In fact the term 'Silk Road' emerges as a pre modern concept, coined by a German geologist Baron Ferdinand von Richtofen in 1877 to describe ancient past.[4] Tasked with mapping routes, he drew five volumes of atlas depicting places in within China and route map connecting China to Germany which he called 'The Silk Road'. The etymology of the word Silk Road itself explains the prism through which the geologist had viewed the route.

Silk, was a textile produced initially in ancient China around 2,700 BC. It was regarded as a high value product reserved for making clothes, drapes and other items to showcase prestige and novelty produced exclusively in China. Since China had monopoly over the luxurious fabric, it enjoyed a favorable place in the exchange network. One of the earliest sources that mentions Silk as commodity is 'Natural History' by *Pliny the elder*, as he mentions Rome imported commodities from China like silk, frankincense, amber and tortoiseshell so much that it was actually weakening the economy. The Chinese used Silk as a diplomatic gift, which became so popular that "Imperial edicts were issued to control its prices in Roman Empire."[5]

Despite the over emphasis, the exchange network was not driven by silk alone, as it was just one of the commodities used for exchange. It is difficult to say which commodity dominated in the exchange network, as it was more of a barter system where one commodity was exchanged for another; for instance Roman silver was used as a form of exchange for silk rather than using it as money for buying Silk. Commodities such as spices, jade, ivory, glass, silver, cotton were equally significant and often dominated the trade network. This posits that neither was the Silk Road an ancient concept nor the Silk Road was used exclusively to trade Silk.

Notwithstanding, it does not mean that there was no movement and exchange in ancient times, it rather means that the terminology used to explain the network is relatively 'new'. Human beings have always moved from one place to another, resulting exchange of ideas, goods and skills. The earliest evidence of the exchange network goes back to 5000 B.C.[6] However, in ancient times there was no particular name or specific route that people followed rather there were a variety of routes and ways that facilitated initial human interaction. Maritime routes were important part of the exchange network as they linked east to west through the sea and have played a crucial role in enabling the exchange of ideas and thoughts.

In fact, maritime routes were more favorable as transportation by land marked by boundaries and power was prone to attacks and looting. The earliest evidences showcasing maritime contact goes thousand years back, the depiction of boats on Harappan and Mesopotamian seals. The archeological finds of wooden boats fastened up by coconut coir further asserts the use of boats even before the use of iron.[7] The early age saw the expansion of the maritime route across the Arabian Sea and gradually entered into the Indian Ocean. Chinese engagement in overseas network can be traced back to the Zhou dynasty (1046-256 B.C.E.). However, it was during the Han and Qin dynasty that the maritime route connecting east to west was formed.[8]

The ancient maritime silk route was divided into two routes: East China Sea Route or "lands above the wind" and South China Sea Route "lands below the wind". The East China Sea Route connected China to Japan and Korea can be dated back to 1112 B.C., while, the South China Sea Route connected it to further East passing through the straits of Malacca, South China sea, the Java sea.[9] The terms were probably used in reference to the wind pattern and the seasons of sailing.

Figure 1: An ancient map of the Maritime Silk Roads/ Quanzhou Municipality

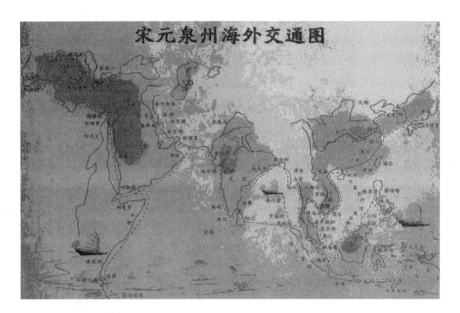

宋元泉州海外交通图

Source: UNESCO

The greatest attraction of insular South Asia was precious spices; maritime routes were used, particularly for transportation spices, supplying markets across the world with cinnamon, pepper, ginger and cloves. Southeast Asia was regarded as 'Survarnabhumi' it might have meant real gold or maybe was used to as a metaphor to equate the profit earned through the spice trade. Indonesia was the hub of these spices known as Spice Island (Malay) back then and the maritime route connecting east and west by the sea was called Spice route as driving force behind the network was spices.[10] Spices such as cinnamon and cassia were traded as early as 2000BC and Egyptians used it medicinally and even rituals.[11] Even Pliny in his writings mentions the importance and trade of cinnamon during the first century.

Recently, Chinese Foreign Minister Spokesperson Hua Chunying in a press conference on 15 March, 2015 highlighted the key elements of the MSR as policy co-ordination, connectivity, trade and investment, people-to-people links and financing development. Three out five inclined towards soft power and use historical assertions as their foundation.[12] A closer look at proposed 21st century MSR will help us to understand the grand strategy and its historical underpinnings.

The way China is projecting its 21st century Maritime Silk Road its inclination is bending more and more towards "the South China Sea Route" leaving the former "East China Sea Route" ignored, highlights the prejudices and inherent biases in the concept itself. Even though the recent initiatives by China is revisiting history and reshaping it, however, the thematic framework used has its own implication and offers a limited scope. The pathway of using Maritime Silk Route (MSR) to understand maritime past reinforces the connotation of European history, as it overlooks the role and importance of commodities other than silk. Lately it has been called 'China's maritime Renaissance'as the attributes and characteristics are indeed Chinese in nature.

Indian initiative: Project Mausam

India under the new leadership has launched Project *Mausam*, an initiative by the Ministry of Culture with Indira Gandhi National Centre for the Arts to acknowledge and celebrate maritime heritage sites across the world. It aims to establish and nominate Indian coastal sites as transnational property on the World Heritage List of UNESCO.[13] Though it might be perceived as a counter to China's MSR, project Mausam is a gradual outcome of historical intervention to identity Indian peninsula within the wider Indian Ocean world.

The idea of organizing and exploring the study of India's cultural relation with the outside world was laid by Greater India Society in 1926.[14] Project Mausam is a result of serious interdisciplinary academic enquiry by researchers to explore Indian Ocean culture, both historically and spaciously. As the blueprint of the project points out the aim of the project is at the macro level to 'reconnect and reestablish communications between the countries of the world, leading to an enhanced understanding of cultural values' and at the micro level it attempts to elaborate and illustrate 'national cultures in their regional maritime milieu'.[15] The historical influence and impact of sea cannot be derived unless and until it has human interaction, for instance, there is no 'history of sea or ocean'[16] as such, and it is always from the human perspective that its dominance or even presence is addressed.

The word 'mausam' was first used by an Arab traveller referring to Arabian Sea later on it was developed and understood as a regular wind system or a season of shipping and navigation by Greeks. Their regular, predictable appearance made them critical for sailors as well as farmers who tilled the land. The 'discovery' of regularity of monsoon winds facilitated easy movement of people, goods and ideas across the Indian Ocean. The occurrence of monsoon winds followed a regular pattern of southwest from May to September and northeast from November to March.

From November to March high pressure builds up over continental Asia and blows dry winds down from Arabia and western India towards Africa and China. The Northeast Monsoon accompanied by surface currents accelerated movement of ships from North to South of Indian Ocean. The winds moves west across the Indian Ocean from Australia to northern Madagascar and then back in a more northerly steam towards Java.

Figure 2: North East Monsoon

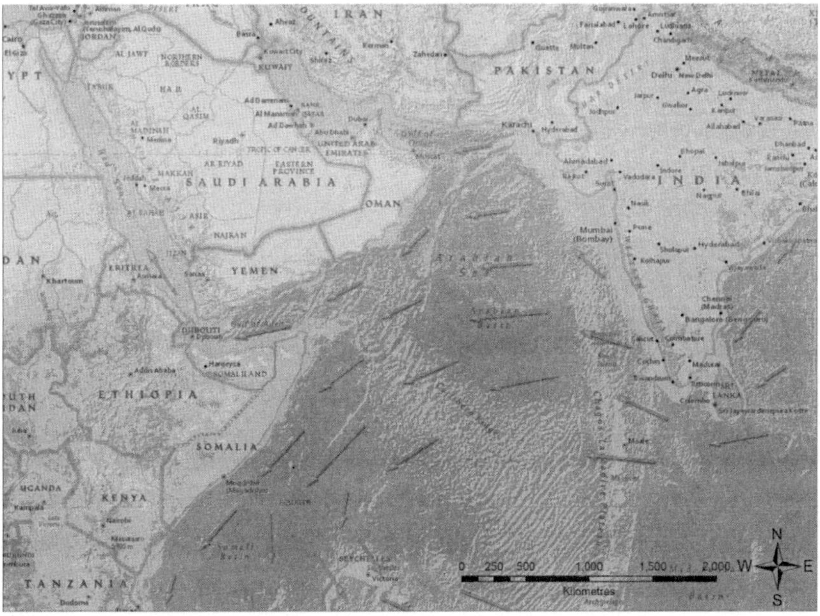

Source: *ESRI & National Geographic*

From May to September this process is reversed, as high pressure zones in the southern hemisphere, accompanied by surface currents pushes strong winds towards the north. This brings heavy rainfall to South and Southwest Asia, the winds blows so strongly in June and July all the sailings were interrupted and the ports were usually closed.

Figure 3: Southwest Monsoon

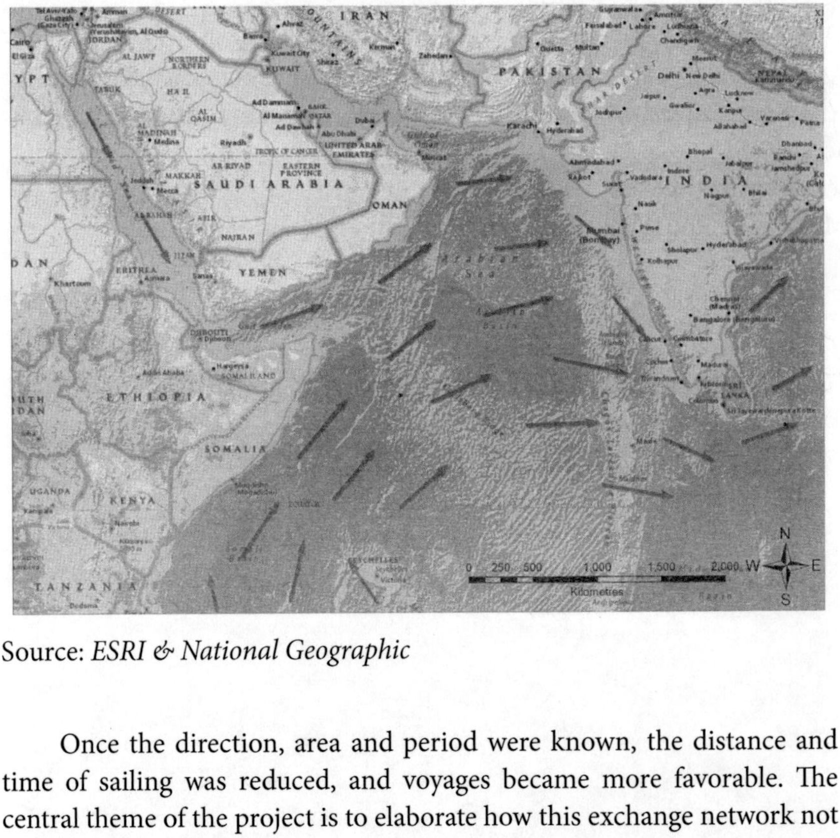

Source: *ESRI & National Geographic*

Once the direction, area and period were known, the distance and time of sailing was reduced, and voyages became more favorable. The central theme of the project is to elaborate how this exchange network not only led to the exchange of commodities, culture, religion, ideas, values and technology, but played a crucial role in influencing patterns of migration, identity formation and cultural changes.

The first National Conference of Project Mausam held in November, 2014, in Kerala highlighted its main objective to review existing material, database, archeological remains in collaboration with various organizations and institutions to evaluate and acknowledge the maritime engagements in the past. The multidisciplinary approach initiated by the project, marked by the intersection of archeology, anthropology, geography and economy, aided by molecular science, oceanology, and meteorology enable to reconstruct understanding of the maritime past and acknowledge it as a global phenomenon at different time and spaces.

Reviewing the maritime past, the project aims to connect local and regional histories in shaping 'the global world' and provides a platform for local and regional researchers to bring forth their work to a common platform. The monthly lecture series of Project Mausam gives scholars across the world, a chance to showcase their study leading to improve accessibility and dissemination of knowledge across the Indian Ocean region. Few issues highlighted in the recent lectures are how movements caused by human activities amalgamated local traditions with the foreign identities and created new forms of art and belief,[17] the need to synthesize material remain and textual sources as of socio-cultural significance,[18] the study of shipwrecks in identifying the scale and complexity of commercial exchange. The study of ship architecture of the vessels adds a further dimension to research, bringing alive the Arabic and Chinese sources which provide meaning and descriptions of this trade.[19]

The holistic approach gives a broader framework for analysis and understanding about the past as a process of social formation, cultural exchange and global economy and enables to study patterns of migration, spread of ideas, rectification and transformation of religion, evolving technologies, evolution of medicine and the spread of diseases. The forgotten and neglected issues of the trade network like indentured labour and the slave trade also get highlighted. The Project initiated by Ministry of Culture aims to explore multiculturalism in the Indian Ocean world by exploring common heritages and the multiple identities nations share. The seminars and conferences held under Project Mausam promotes scholars to study 'shared past' by generating a multitude of themes that it incorporates.

Though the project highlights several aspects of the maritime past, however many more remain. The trade ties and exchange relation were not entirely sea borne there were instances of overland ties as well that ensured smooth circulation of goods and commodities. The overseas maritime trade could have never flourished without a well-established overland trade network. The way project has been shaping up, it has overlooked the role of regional linkages in establishing overseas ties. This makes the project a little rigid and leaves a very little space for any elaborative understanding of cultural engagement and linkages between the coast and hinterland. The regional and local ties were crucial as, not everything traded was produced in coastal areas. The study of regional ties will enable us to understand the organization and adaptability of a trading network, the regional linkages of trade, pattern of migration and its impact.

The epistemological approach initiated by project Mausam helps us to break away from the conventional conjecture of continental histories and allows a 'representation independent reality,'[20] an understanding of the historical past as an inclusive connecting process. This gives a broader framework for analysis and understanding about the past as a process of social formation, cultural exchange and global economy.

Convergences and Divergences

The twenty-first century initiatives by India and China have brought much limelight to 'matters maritime'. In the present global scenario, the contemporary issues and standings of both the countries are evoking knowledge of the past. The MSR and project Mausam recall maritime history and revisit maritime past to show their assertive participation in the overseas exchange network. Both initiatives are taken by two of the largest countries of Asia and can also be seen as an outcome of the rise of Asia.

Though both might have the same manure, the basic thrust is conflicting as MSR attempts to 'build a modern Maritime Silk Road' while Mausam aims to 'preserve and acknowledge the ancient linkages'. MSR has a limited connotation and follows a set pattern of exchange network, however Mausam isn't necessarily driven by any specific route or path rather it traces a variety of routes and paths followed by traders, merchants, expeditionary, explorers, missionaries, etc. Giving the holistic understanding of 'matters maritime' the projects explores oceanic exchanges as a process throughout the past. This inclusive approach initiated by Project Mausam enables us to explore various aspects of overseas exchange like, patterns of migration, spread of ideas, rectification and transformation of religion, evolving technologies, evolution of medicine and the spread of diseases.

The way MSR is shaping up, it is constricted by the ideological framework of using a 'modern or rather nationalist terminology' to define a process that dates back to antiquity. The ideological barrier of the 'Silk Road' is constricted in scope as it carries its own baggage's and overlooks the role and importance of other commodities such as spices, silver, iron, brass, etc. The usage of the term 'Silk Road' can be seen as China's attempt to certify dominance in maritime exchange network, as silk was the commodity over which China had monopoly for long. Also, the inclination of MSR towards South China Sea Route leaves the former ignored. Disregarding the role and importance of the East China Sea Route, the epistemological inquiry initiated by China has a strong political character. The attributes Chinese are attaching to the South China Sea route will enable them to do historical research and thus will have a greater influence in the South China Route. This could be understood as what historians call as 'Silencing the Past'[21]. The use of power can not only be derived from political structure, economic standing, but also, the way and means of viewing the past. In this case the way China is deliberately using the power and authority to redefine historical linkages and reshape the history.

Findings

The initiatives by both India and China to revisit history, cannot be denied of having a strategic intent. The way China is promoting its 21st century MSR by building roads, railway, ports across the South Asia and even beyond, will enable it to have greater influence and access. India's Project Mausam emerges to rather be more holistic as it intents to initiate the dissemination of knowledge by equal participation across the Indian Ocean region. However, both the initiatives can be seen in similar shades. Both the concepts should be understood in context of the present global scenario as the historical approach by both the countries can be seen as an attempt to enhance their presence in the maritime domain.

Despite, a few fallouts the 21st century approach of mutual cooperation and collaboration to revisit maritime past emerges as an asset, highlighting the connecting histories, it recognizes past as a shared space. This will enable us to acknowledge the vastness and complexity of the oceans, not just geographically, socially and politically.

Notes and References

1   "China says 'Mausam' can be linked to One Belt One Road." *Deccan Herald*, 05 March 2015, National section http://www.deccanherald.com/content/463755/china-says-mausam-can-linked.html. Also see, VR, Srinivasan. "Building ties for 21ˢᵗ century." *The Hindu*, 01 April 2015, http://www.thehindu.com/todays-paper/tp-opinion/building-ties-for-the-21st-century/article7055231.ece, (accessed 19 February 2015).

2   *China Highlights*, "Silk Road" http://www.chinahighlights.com/silkroad/history.htm (accessed 19 February 2015).

3   Ibid.

4   *UNESCO Silk Road Dialogue Diversity and Development*, "About the Silk Road," https://en.unesco.org/silkroad/about-silk-road (accessed 21 March 2015).

5   Ibid.

6   Edward Alpers, *The Indian Ocean in World History* (Oxford: Oxford University Press, 2014), p. 23.

7   Himanshu Prabha Ray and J.F. Salles, *Tradition and Archeology* (Delhi: Manohar, 1996), p.5.

8   'Silk Road', Note 2.

9   John N Miksic, *Singapore and the Silk Road of the Sea, 1300-1800* (Singapore; NUS Press, 2013) p.37. Also see, 'Travel Guide,' Maritime Silk Road, *China Highlights*, http://www.chinahighlights.com/travelguide/maritime-silk-road.htm, (accessed 19 February 2015).

10   About the Silk Road, Note 4.

11   Alpers, Note 6, p.32.

12   Hua Chunying, Foreign Ministry Spokesperson. http://sc.china-embassy.org/eng/fyrth/t1128254.htm,(Press Confrence at Seychelles, Feburary 13, 2014; (accessed 15 March 2015).

13   *Indira Gandhi National Centre for the Arts*, "Project Mausam Concept Note" http://ignca.nic.in/mausam/Mausam_Concept.pdf (accessed 05 Decemeber 2014).

14   Kwa Chong-Guan et al., *Early Southeast Asia viewed from India: An anthology of articles from the Journal of the Greater India Society* (New Delhi; Manohar Publishers & Distributors, 2013).

15 "Project Mausam Concept Note", Note 13.

16 Ashin Das Gupta and M.N.Pearson, *India and the Indian Ocean 1500-1800* (New Delhi, : Oxford University Press, 1987), p. 27.

17 Osmund Bopearachichi, "Maritime Trade and Cultural Exchange in the Indian Ocean: India and Sri Lanka" (Paper presented for monthly lecture series of Project Mausam at Indira Gandhi National Centre for the Arts, New Delhi, India, 30 December 2014).

18 Mayur Babulal Thakare, "Indo-European Defence Architecture in North Konkan, 1510-1818" (Paper presented for monthly lecture series of Project Mausam at Indira Gandhi National Centre for the Arts, New Delhi, India, 04 June 2014).

19 John Guy, "Emporiums of Indian Ocean Trade, witnessed by the Java Sea Shipwrecks of the 9th and 10th Centuries." (Paper presented for monthly lecture series of Project Mausam at Indira Gandhi National Centre for the Arts, New Delhi, India, 09 February 2015).

20 Daniel Little, *Contributions to the Philosophy of History* (Dordrecht; Springer Science, 2010), p. 15.

21 Michel-Rolph Trouillot, *Silencing The Past: Power And Production Of History.* (Boston; Mass: Beacon Press, 1995).

Vision and Actions on Jointly Building Silk Road Economic Belt and 21st-Century Maritime Silk Road

(Issued by the National Development and Reform Commission, Ministry of Foreign Affairs, and Ministry of Commerce of the People's Republic of China, with State Council authorization, 28 March 2015, First Edition)

(Weblink- http://en.ndrc.gov.cn/newsrelease/201503/t20150330_669367.html)

Preface

More than two millennia ago the diligent and courageous people of Eurasia explored and opened up several routes of trade and cultural exchanges that linked the major civilizations of Asia, Europe and Africa, collectively called the Silk Road by later generations. For thousands of years, the Silk Road Spirit – "peace and cooperation, openness and inclusiveness, mutual learning and mutual benefit" – has been passed from generation to generation, promoted the progress of human civilization, and contributed greatly to the prosperity and development of the countries along the Silk Road. Symbolizing communication and cooperation between the East and the West, the Silk Road Spirit is a historic and cultural heritage shared by all countries around the world.

In the 21st century, a new era marked by the theme of peace, development, cooperation and mutual benefit, it is all the more important for us to carry on the Silk Road Spirit in face of the weak recovery of the global economy, and complex international and regional situations.

When Chinese President Xi Jinping visited Central Asia and Southeast Asia in September and October of 2013, he raised the initiative of jointly building the Silk Road Economic Belt and the 21st-Century Maritime Silk Road (hereinafter referred to as the Belt and Road), which have attracted close attention from all over the world. At the China-ASEAN Expo in 2013, Chinese Premier Li Keqiang emphasized the need to build the Maritime Silk Road oriented towards ASEAN, and to create strategic propellers for hinterland development. Accelerating the building of the Belt and Road can help promote the economic prosperity of the countries along the Belt and Road and regional economic cooperation, strengthen exchanges and mutual learning between different civilizations, and promote world peace and development. It is a great undertaking that will benefit people around the world.

The Belt and Road Initiative is a systematic project, which should be jointly built through consultation to meet the interests of all, and efforts should be made to integrate the development strategies of the countries along the Belt and Road. The Chinese government has drafted and published the Vision and Actions on Jointly Building Silk Road Economic Belt and 21st-Century Maritime Silk Road to promote the implementation of the Initiative, instill vigor and vitality into the ancient Silk Road, connect Asian, European and African countries more closely and promote mutually beneficial cooperation to a new high and in new forms.

I. Background

Complex and profound changes are taking place in the world. The underlying impact of the international financial crisis keeps emerging; the world economy is recovering slowly, and global development is uneven; the international trade and investment landscape and rules for multilateral trade and investment are undergoing major adjustments; and countries still face big challenges to their development.

The initiative to jointly build the Belt and Road, embracing the trend towards a multipolar world, economic globalization, cultural diversity and greater IT application, is designed to uphold the global free trade regime and the open world economy in the spirit of open regional cooperation. It is aimed at promoting orderly and free flow of economic factors, highly efficient allocation of resources and deep integration of markets; encouraging the countries along the Belt and Road to achieve economic policy coordination and carry out broader and more in-depth regional cooperation of higher standards; and jointly creating an open, inclusive and balanced regional economic cooperation architecture that benefits all. Jointly building the Belt and Road is in the interests of the world community. Reflecting the common ideals and pursuit of human societies, it is a positive endeavor to seek new models of international cooperation and global governance, and will inject new positive energy into world peace and development.

The Belt and Road Initiative aims to promote the connectivity of Asian, European and African continents and their adjacent seas, establish and strengthen partnerships among the countries along the Belt and Road, set up all-dimensional, multi-tiered and composite connectivity networks, and realize diversified, independent, balanced and sustainable development in these countries. The connectivity projects of the Initiative will help align and coordinate the development strategies of the countries along the Belt and Road, tap market potential in this region, promote investment and consumption, create demands and job opportunities, enhance people-to-people and cultural exchanges, and mutual learning among the peoples of the relevant countries, and enable them to understand, trust and respect each other and live in harmony, peace and prosperity.

China's economy is closely connected with the world economy. China will stay committed to the basic policy of opening-up, build a new pattern of all-round opening-up, and integrate itself deeper into the world economic system. The Initiative will enable China to further expand and deepen its opening-up, and to strengthen its mutually beneficial cooperation with countries in Asia, Europe and Africa and the rest of the world. China is committed to shouldering more responsibilities and obligations within its capabilities, and making greater contributions to the peace and development of mankind.

II. Principles

The Belt and Road Initiative is in line with the purposes and principles of the UN Charter. It upholds the Five Principles of Peaceful Coexistence: mutual respect for each other's sovereignty and territorial integrity, mutual non-aggression, mutual non-interference in each other's internal affairs, equality and mutual benefit, and peaceful coexistence.

The Initiative is open for cooperation. It covers, but is not limited to, the area of the ancient Silk Road. It is open to all countries, and international and regional organizations for engagement, so that the results of the concerted efforts will benefit wider areas.

The Initiative is harmonious and inclusive. It advocates tolerance among civilizations, respects the paths and modes of development chosen by different countries, and supports dialogues among different civilizations on the principles of seeking common ground while shelving differences and drawing on each other's strengths, so that all countries can coexist in peace for common prosperity.

The Initiative follows market operation. It will abide by market rules and international norms, give play to the decisive role of the market in resource allocation and the primary role of enterprises, and let the governments perform their due functions.

The Initiative seeks mutual benefit. It accommodates the interests and concerns of all parties involved, and seeks a conjunction of interests and the "biggest common denominator" for cooperation so as to give full play to the wisdom and creativity, strengths and potentials of all parties.

III. Framework

The Belt and Road Initiative is a way for win-win cooperation that promotes common development and prosperity and a road towards peace and friendship by enhancing mutual understanding and trust, and strengthening all-round exchanges. The Chinese government advocates peace and cooperation, openness and inclusiveness, mutual learning and mutual benefit. It promotes practical cooperation in all fields, and works to build a community of shared interests, destiny and responsibility featuring mutual political trust, economic integration and cultural inclusiveness.

The Belt and Road run through the continents of Asia, Europe and Africa, connecting the vibrant East Asia economic circle at one end and developed European economic circle at the other, and encompassing countries with huge potential for economic development. The Silk Road Economic Belt focuses on bringing together China, Central Asia, Russia and Europe (the Baltic); linking China with the Persian Gulf and the Mediterranean Sea through Central Asia and West Asia; and connecting China with Southeast Asia, South Asia and the Indian Ocean. The 21st-Century Maritime Silk Road is designed to go from China's coast to Europe through the South China Sea and the Indian Ocean in one route, and from China's coast through the South China Sea to the South Pacific in the other.

On land, the Initiative will focus on jointly building a new Eurasian Land Bridge and developing China-Mongolia-Russia, China-Central Asia-

West Asia and China-Indochina Peninsula economic corridors by taking advantage of international transport routes, relying on core cities along the Belt and Road and using key economic industrial parks as cooperation platforms. At sea, the Initiative will focus on jointly building smooth, secure and efficient transport routes connecting major sea ports along the Belt and Road. The China-Pakistan Economic Corridor and the Bangladesh-China-India-Myanmar Economic Corridor are closely related to the Belt and Road Initiative, and therefore require closer cooperation and greater progress.

The Initiative is an ambitious economic vision of the opening-up of and cooperation among the countries along the Belt and Road. Countries should work in concert and move towards the objectives of mutual benefit and common security. To be specific, they need to improve the region's infrastructure, and put in place a secure and efficient network of land, sea and air passages, lifting their connectivity to a higher level; further enhance trade and investment facilitation, establish a network of free trade areas that meet high standards, maintain closer economic ties, and deepen political trust; enhance cultural exchanges; encourage different civilizations to learn from each other and flourish together; and promote mutual understanding, peace and friendship among people of all countries.

IV. Cooperation Priorities

Countries along the Belt and Road have their own resource advantages and their economies are mutually complementary. Therefore, there is a great potential and space for cooperation. They should promote policy coordination, facilities connectivity, unimpeded trade, financial integration and people-to-people bonds as their five major goals, and strengthen cooperation in the following key areas:

Policy coordination

Enhancing policy coordination is an important guarantee for implementing the Initiative. We should promote intergovernmental cooperation, build a multi-level intergovernmental macro policy exchange and communication mechanism, expand shared interests, enhance mutual political trust, and reach new cooperation consensus. Countries along the Belt and Road may fully coordinate their economic development strategies and policies, work out plans and measures for regional cooperation, negotiate to solve cooperation-related issues, and jointly provide policy support for the implementation of practical cooperation and large-scale projects.

Facilities connectivity

Facilities connectivity is a priority area for implementing the Initiative. On the basis of respecting each other's sovereignty and security concerns, countries along the Belt and Road should improve the connectivity of their infrastructure construction plans and technical standard systems, jointly push forward the construction of international trunk passageways, and form an infrastructure network connecting all sub-regions in Asia, and between Asia, Europe and Africa step by step. At the same time, efforts should be made to promote green and low-carbon infrastructure construction and operation management, taking into full account the impact of climate change on the construction.

With regard to transport infrastructure construction, we should focus on the key passageways, junctions and projects, and give priority to linking up unconnected road sections, removing transport bottlenecks, advancing road safety facilities and traffic management facilities and equipment, and improving road network connectivity. We should build a unified coordination mechanism for whole-course transportation, increase connectivity of customs clearance, reloading and multimodal transport between countries, and gradually formulate compatible and standard transport rules, so as to realize international transport facilitation. We should push forward port infrastructure construction, build smooth land-water transportation channels, and advance port cooperation; increase sea routes and the number of voyages, and enhance information technology cooperation in maritime logistics. We should expand and build platforms and mechanisms for comprehensive civil aviation cooperation, and quicken our pace in improving aviation infrastructure.

We should promote cooperation in the connectivity of energy infrastructure, work in concert to ensure the security of oil and gas pipelines and other transport routes, build cross-border power supply networks and power-transmission routes, and cooperate in regional power grid upgrading and transformation.

We should jointly advance the construction of cross-border optical cables and other communications trunk line networks, improve international communications connectivity, and create an Information Silk Road. We should build bilateral cross-border optical cable networks at a quicker pace, plan transcontinental submarine optical cable projects, and improve spatial (satellite) information passageways to expand information exchanges and cooperation.

Unimpeded trade

Investment and trade cooperation is a major task in building the Belt and Road. We should strive to improve investment and trade facilitation, and remove investment and trade barriers for the creation of a sound business environment within the region and in all related countries. We will discuss with countries and regions along the Belt and Road on opening free trade areas so as to unleash the potential for expanded cooperation.

Countries along the Belt and Road should enhance customs cooperation such as information exchange, mutual recognition of regulations, and mutual assistance in law enforcement; improve bilateral and multilateral cooperation in the fields of inspection and quarantine, certification and accreditation, standard measurement, and statistical information; and work to ensure that the WTO Trade Facilitation Agreement takes effect and is implemented. We should improve the customs clearance facilities of border ports, establish a "single-window" in border ports, reduce customs clearance costs, and improve customs clearance capability. We should increase cooperation in supply chain safety and convenience, improve the coordination of cross-border supervision procedures, promote online checking of inspection and quarantine certificates, and facilitate mutual recognition of Authorized Economic Operators. We should lower non-tariff barriers, jointly improve the transparency of technical trade measures, and enhance trade liberalization and facilitation.

We should expand trading areas, improve trade structure, explore new growth areas of trade, and promote trade balance. We should make innovations in our forms of trade, and develop cross-border e-commerce and other modern business models. A service trade support system should be set up to consolidate and expand conventional trade, and efforts to develop modern service trade should be strengthened. We should integrate investment and trade, and promote trade through investment.

We should speed up investment facilitation, eliminate investment barriers, and push forward negotiations on bilateral investment protection agreements and double taxation avoidance agreements to protect the lawful rights and interests of investors.

We should expand mutual investment areas, deepen cooperation in agriculture, forestry, animal husbandry and fisheries, agricultural machinery manufacturing and farm produce processing, and promote cooperation in marine-product farming, deep-sea fishing, aquatic product processing, seawater desalination, marine biopharmacy, ocean engineering technology, environmental protection industries, marine tourism and other fields. We should increase cooperation in the exploration and development of coal, oil, gas, metal minerals and other conventional energy sources; advance cooperation in hydropower, nuclear power, wind power, solar power and other clean, renewable energy sources; and promote cooperation in the processing and conversion of energy and resources at or near places where they are exploited, so as to create an integrated industrial chain of energy and resource cooperation. We should enhance cooperation in deep-processing technology, equipment and engineering services in the fields of energy and resources.

We should push forward cooperation in emerging industries. In accordance with the principles of mutual complementarity and mutual benefit, we should promote in-depth cooperation with other countries along the Belt and Road in new-generation information technology, biotechnology, new energy technology, new materials and other emerging industries, and establish entrepreneurial and investment cooperation mechanisms.

We should improve the division of labor and distribution of industrial chains by encouraging the entire industrial chain and related industries to develop in concert; establish R&D, production and marketing systems; and improve industrial supporting capacity and the overall competitiveness of regional industries. We should increase the openness of our service industry to each other to accelerate the development of regional service industries. We should explore a new mode of investment cooperation, working together to build all forms of industrial parks such as overseas economic and trade cooperation zones and cross-border economic cooperation zones, and promote industrial cluster development. We should promote ecological progress in conducting investment and trade, increase cooperation in conserving eco-environment, protecting biodiversity, and tackling climate change, and join hands to make the Silk Road an environment-friendly one.

We welcome companies from all countries to invest in China, and encourage Chinese enterprises to participate in infrastructure construction in other countries along the Belt and Road, and make industrial investments there. We support localized operation and management of Chinese companies to boost the local economy, increase local employment, improve local livelihood, and take social responsibilities in protecting local biodiversity and eco-environment.

Financial integration

Financial integration is an important underpinning for implementing the Belt and Road Initiative. We should deepen financial cooperation, and make more efforts in building a currency stability system, investment and financing system and credit information system in Asia. We should expand the scope and scale of bilateral currency swap and settlement with other countries along the Belt and Road, open and develop the bond market in Asia, make joint efforts to establish the Asian Infrastructure Investment Bank and BRICS New Development Bank, conduct negotiation among related parties on establishing Shanghai Cooperation Organization (SCO) financing institution, and set up and put into operation the Silk Road Fund as early as possible. We should strengthen practical cooperation of China-ASEAN Interbank Association and SCO Interbank Association, and carry out multilateral financial cooperation in the form of syndicated loans and bank credit. We will support the efforts of governments of the countries along the Belt and Road and their companies and financial institutions with good credit-rating to issue Renminbi bonds in China. Qualified Chinese financial institutions and companies are encouraged to issue bonds in both Renminbi and foreign currencies outside China, and use the funds thus collected in countries along the Belt and Road.

We should strengthen financial regulation cooperation, encourage the signing of MOUs on cooperation in bilateral financial regulation, and establish an efficient regulation coordination mechanism in the region. We should improve the system of risk response and crisis management, build a regional financial risk early-warning system, and create an exchange and cooperation mechanism of addressing cross-border risks and crisis. We should increase cross-border exchange and cooperation between credit investigation regulators, credit investigation institutions and credit rating institutions. We should give full play to the role of the Silk Road Fund and that of sovereign wealth funds of countries along the Belt and Road, and encourage commercial equity investment funds and private funds to participate in the construction of key projects of the Initiative.

People-to-people bond

People-to-people bond provides the public support for implementing the Initiative. We should carry forward the spirit of friendly cooperation of the Silk Road by promoting extensive cultural and academic exchanges, personnel exchanges and cooperation, media cooperation, youth and women exchanges and volunteer services, so as to win public support for deepening bilateral and multilateral cooperation.

We should send more students to each other's countries, and promote cooperation in jointly running schools. China provides 10,000 government scholarships to the countries along the Belt and Road every year. We should hold culture years, arts festivals, film festivals, TV weeks and book fairs in each other's countries; cooperate on the production and translation of fine films, radio and TV programs; and jointly apply for and protect World Cultural Heritage sites. We should also increase personnel exchange and cooperation between countries along the Belt and Road.

We should enhance cooperation in and expand the scale of tourism; hold tourism promotion weeks and publicity months in each other's countries; jointly create competitive international tourist routes and products with Silk Road features; and make it more convenient to apply for tourist visa in countries along the Belt and Road. We should push forward cooperation on the 21st-Century Maritime Silk Road cruise tourism program. We should carry out sports exchanges and support countries along the Belt and Road in their bid for hosting major international sports events.

We should strengthen cooperation with neighboring countries on epidemic information sharing, the exchange of prevention and treatment technologies and the training of medical professionals, and improve our capability to jointly address public health emergencies. We will provide medical assistance and emergency medical aid to relevant countries, and carry out practical cooperation in maternal and child health, disability rehabilitation, and major infectious diseases including AIDS, tuberculosis and malaria. We will also expand cooperation on traditional medicine.

We should increase our cooperation in science and technology, establish joint labs (or research centers), international technology transfer centers and maritime cooperation centers, promote sci-tech personnel exchanges, cooperate in tackling key sci-tech problems, and work together to improve sci-tech innovation capability.

We should integrate existing resources to expand and advance practical cooperation between countries along the Belt and Road on youth employment, entrepreneurship training, vocational skill development, social security management, public administration and management and in other areas of common interest.

We should give full play to the bridging role of communication between political parties and parliaments, and promote friendly exchanges between legislative bodies, major political parties and political organizations of countries along the Belt and Road. We should carry out exchanges and cooperation among cities, encourage major cities in these countries to become sister cities, focus on promoting practical cooperation, particularly cultural and people-to-people exchanges, and create more lively examples of cooperation. We welcome the think tanks in the countries along the Belt and Road to jointly conduct research and hold forums.

We should increase exchanges and cooperation between non-governmental organizations of countries along the Belt and Road, organize public interest activities concerning education, health care, poverty reduction, biodiversity and ecological protection for the benefit of the general public, and improve the production and living conditions of poverty-stricken areas along the Belt and Road. We should enhance international exchanges and cooperation on culture and media, and leverage the positive role of the Internet and new media tools to foster harmonious and friendly cultural environment and public opinion.

V. Cooperation Mechanisms

The world economic integration is accelerating and regional cooperation is on the upswing. China will take full advantage of the existing bilateral and multilateral cooperation mechanisms to push forward the building of the

Belt and Road and to promote the development of regional cooperation.

We should strengthen bilateral cooperation, and promote comprehensive development of bilateral relations through multi-level and multi-channel communication and consultation. We should encourage the signing of cooperation MOUs or plans, and develop a number of bilateral cooperation pilot projects. We should establish and improve bilateral joint working mechanisms, and draw up implementation plans and roadmaps for advancing the Belt and Road Initiative. In addition, we should give full play to the existing bilateral mechanisms such as joint committee, mixed committee, coordinating committee, steering committee and management committee to coordinate and promote the implementation of cooperation projects.

We should enhance the role of multilateral cooperation mechanisms, make full use of existing mechanisms such as the Shanghai Cooperation Organization (SCO), ASEAN Plus China (10+1), Asia-Pacific Economic Cooperation (APEC), Asia-Europe Meeting (ASEM), Asia Cooperation Dialogue (ACD), Conference on Interaction and Confidence-Building Measures in Asia (CICA), China-Arab States Cooperation Forum (CASCF), China-Gulf Cooperation Council Strategic Dialogue, Greater Mekong Sub-region (GMS) Economic Cooperation, and Central Asia Regional Economic Cooperation (CAREC) to strengthen communication with relevant countries, and attract more countries and regions to participate in the Belt and Road Initiative.

We should continue to encourage the constructive role of the international forums and exhibitions at regional and sub-regional levels hosted by countries along the Belt and Road, as well as such platforms as Boao Forum for Asia, China-ASEAN Expo, China-Eurasia Expo, Euro-Asia Economic Forum, China International Fair for Investment and Trade, China-South Asia Expo, China-Arab States Expo, Western China International Fair, China-Russia Expo, and Qianhai Cooperation Forum. We should support the local authorities and general public of countries along the Belt and Road to explore the historical and cultural heritage of the Belt and Road, jointly hold investment, trade and cultural exchange activities, and ensure the success of the Silk Road (Dunhuang) International Culture Expo, Silk Road International Film Festival and Silk Road International Book Fair. We propose to set up an international summit forum on the Belt and Road Initiative.

VI. China's Regions in Pursuing Opening-Up

In advancing the Belt and Road Initiative, China will fully leverage the comparative advantages of its various regions, adopt a proactive strategy of further opening-up, strengthen interaction and cooperation among the eastern, western and central regions, and comprehensively improve the openness of the Chinese economy.

Northwestern and northeastern regions. We should make good use of Xinjiang's geographic advantages and its role as a window of westward opening-up to deepen communication and cooperation with Central, South and West Asian countries, make it a key transportation, trade, logistics, culture, science and education center, and a core area on the Silk Road Economic Belt. We should give full scope to the economic and cultural strengths of Shaanxi and Gansu provinces and the ethnic and cultural advantages of the Ningxia Hui Autonomous Region and Qinghai Province, build Xi'an into a new focus of reform and opening-up in China's interior, speed up the development and opening-up of cities such as Lanzhou and Xining, and advance the building of the Ningxia Inland Opening-up Pilot Economic Zone with the goal of creating strategic channels, trade and logistics hubs and key bases for industrial and cultural exchanges opening to Central, South and West Asian countries. We should give full play to Inner Mongolia's proximity to Mongolia and Russia, improve the railway links connecting Heilongjiang Province with Russia and the regional railway network, strengthen cooperation between China's Heilongjiang, Jilin and Liaoning provinces and Russia's Far East region on sea-land multi-modal transport, and advance the construction of an Eurasian high-speed transport corridor linking Beijing and Moscow with the goal of building key windows opening to the north.

Southwestern region. We should give full play to the unique advantage of Guangxi Zhuang Autonomous Region as a neighbor of ASEAN countries, speed up the opening-up and development of the Beibu Gulf Economic Zone and the Pearl River-Xijiang Economic Zone, build an international corridor opening to the ASEAN region, create new strategic anchors for the opening-up and development of the southwest and mid-south regions of China, and form an important gateway connecting the Silk Road Economic Belt and the 21st-Century Maritime Silk Road. We should make good use of the geographic advantage of Yunnan Province, advance the construction of an international transport corridor connecting China with neighboring countries, develop a new highlight of economic cooperation in the Greater Mekong Sub-region, and make the region a pivot of China's opening-up to South and Southeast Asia. We should promote the border trade and tourism and culture cooperation between Tibet Autonomous Region and neighboring countries such as Nepal.

Coastal regions, and Hong Kong, Macao and Taiwan. We should leverage the strengths of the Yangtze River Delta, Pearl River Delta, west coast of the Taiwan Straits, Bohai Rim, and other areas with economic zones boasting a high level of openness, robust economic strengths and strong catalytic role, speed up the development of the China (Shanghai) Pilot Free Trade Zone, and support Fujian Province in becoming a core area of the 21st-Century Maritime Silk Road. We should give full scope to the role of Qianhai (Shenzhen), Nansha (Guangzhou), Hengqin (Zhuhai) and Pingtan (Fujian) in opening-up and cooperation, deepen their cooperation with Hong Kong, Macao and Taiwan, and help to build the Guangdong-Hong Kong-Macao Big Bay Area. We should promote the development of the Zhejiang Marine Economy Development Demonstration Zone, Fujian Marine Economic Pilot Zone and Zhoushan Archipelago New Area, and further open Hainan Province as an international tourism· island. We should strengthen the port construction of coastal cities such as Shanghai, Tianjin, Ningbo-Zhoushan, Guangzhou, Shenzhen, Zhanjiang, Shantou, Qingdao, Yantai, Dalian, Fuzhou, Xiamen, Quanzhou, Haikou and Sanya, and strengthen the functions of international hub airports such as Shanghai and Guangzhou. We should use opening-up to motivate these areas to carry out deeper reform, create new systems and mechanisms of open economy, step up scientific and technological innovation, develop new advantages for participating in and leading international cooperation and competition, and become the pace-setter and main force in the Belt and Road Initiative, particularly the building of the 21st-Century Maritime Silk Road. We should leverage the unique role of overseas Chinese and the Hong Kong and Macao Special Administrative Regions, and encourage them to participate in and contribute to the Belt and Road Initiative. We should also make proper arrangements for the Taiwan region to be part of this effort.

Inland regions. We should make use of the advantages of inland regions, including a vast landmass, rich human resources and a strong industrial foundation, focus on such key regions as the city clusters along the middle reaches of the Yangtze River, around Chengdu and Chongqing, in central Henan Province, around Hohhot, Baotou, Erdos and Yulin, and around Harbin and Changchun to propel regional interaction and cooperation and industrial concentration. We should build Chongqing into an important pivot for developing and opening up the western region, and make Chengdu, Zhengzhou, Wuhan, Changsha, Nanchang and Hefei leading areas of opening-up in the inland regions. We should accelerate cooperation between regions on the upper and middle reaches of the Yangtze River and their counterparts along Russia's Volga River. We should set up coordination mechanisms in terms of railway transport and port customs clearance for the China-Europe corridor, cultivate the brand of "China-Europe freight trains," and construct a cross-border transport corridor connecting the eastern, central and western regions. We should support inland cities such as Zhengzhou and Xi'an in building airports and international land ports, strengthen customs clearance cooperation between inland ports and ports in the coastal and border regions, and launch pilot e-commerce services for cross-border trade. We should optimize the layout of special customs oversight areas, develop new models of processing trade, and deepen industrial cooperation with countries along the Belt and Road.

VII. China in Action

For more than a year, the Chinese government has been actively promoting the building of the Belt and Road, enhancing communication and consultation and advancing practical cooperation with countries along the Belt and Road, and introduced a series of policies and measures for early outcomes.

High-level guidance and facilitation. President Xi Jinping and Premier Li Keqiang have visited over 20 countries, attended the Dialogue on Strengthening Connectivity Partnership and the sixth ministerial conference of the China-Arab States Cooperation Forum, and met with leaders of relevant countries to discuss bilateral relations and regional development issues. They have used these opportunities to explain the rich contents and positive implications of the Belt and Road Initiative, and their efforts have helped bring about a broad consensus on the Belt and Road Initiative.

Signing cooperation framework. China has signed MOUs of cooperation on the joint development of the Belt and Road with some countries, and on regional cooperation and border cooperation and mid- and long-term development plans for economic and trade cooperation with some neighboring countries. It has proposed outlines of regional cooperation plans with some adjacent countries.

Promoting project cooperation. China has enhanced communication and consultation with countries along the Belt and Road, and promoted a number of key cooperation projects in the fields of infrastructure connectivity, industrial investment, resource development, economic and trade cooperation, financial cooperation, cultural exchanges, ecological protection and maritime cooperation where the conditions are right.

Improving policies and measures. The Chinese government will integrate its domestic resources to provide stronger policy support for the Initiative. It will facilitate the establishment of the Asian Infrastructure Investment Bank. China has proposed the Silk Road Fund, and the investment function of the China-Eurasia Economic Cooperation Fund will be reinforced. We will encourage bank card clearing institutions to conduct cross-border clearing operations, and payment institutions to conduct cross-border payment business. We will actively promote investment and trade facilitation, and accelerate the reform of integrated regional customs clearance.

Boosting the role of cooperation platforms. A number of international summits, forums, seminars and expos on the theme of the Belt and Road Initiative have been held, which have played an important role in increasing mutual understanding, reaching consensus and deepening cooperation.

VIII. Embracing a Brighter Future Together

Though proposed by China, the Belt and Road Initiative is a common aspiration of all countries along their routes. China is ready to conduct equal-footed consultation with all countries along the Belt and Road to seize the opportunity provided by the Initiative, promote opening-up, communication and integration among countries in a larger scope, with higher standards and at deeper levels, while giving consideration to the interests and aspirations of all parties. The development of the Belt and Road is open and inclusive, and we welcome the active participation of all countries and international and regional organizations in this Initiative.

The development of the Belt and Road should mainly be conducted through policy communication and objectives coordination. It is a pluralistic and open process of cooperation which can be highly flexible, and does not seek conformity. China will join other countries along the Belt and Road to substantiate and improve the content and mode of the Belt and Road cooperation, work out relevant timetables and roadmaps, and align national development programs and regional cooperation plans.

China will work with countries along the Belt and Road to carry out joint research, forums and fairs, personnel training, exchanges and visits under the framework of existing bilateral, multilateral, regional and sub-regional cooperation mechanisms, so that they will gain a better understanding and recognition of the contents, objectives and tasks of the Belt and Road Initiative.

China will work with countries along the Belt and Road to steadily advance demonstration projects, jointly identify programs that accommodate bilateral and multilateral interests, and accelerate the launching of programs that are agreed upon by parties and ready for implementation, so as to ensure early harvest.

The Belt and Road cooperation features mutual respect and trust, mutual benefit and win-win cooperation, and mutual learning between civilizations. As long as all countries along the Belt and Road make concerted efforts to pursue our common goal, there will be bright prospects for the Silk Road Economic Belt and the 21st-Century Maritime Silk Road, and the people of countries along the Belt and Road can all benefit from this Initiative.

Index

A

Act East 9, 26

Admiral Zheng He 11, 44

Adwita Rai vi, vii, xv, 111

Air Defence Identification Zone xi, 34

Antara Ghosal Singh v, vii, 80

Anti-Ship Ballistic Missile xi, 32

Asia Cooperation Dialogue (ACD) 136

Asia-Europe Meeting 21, 136

Asian Infrastructure Investment Bank xi, 2, 15, 19, 36, 48, 50, 51, 54, 55, 56, 58, 59, 69, 71, 83, 133, 140

Asia-Pacific Economic Cooperation (APEC) 136

Association of Southeast Asian Nations (ASEAN) xi, xiv, 1, 10, 16, 21, 23, 43, 48, 49, 50, 51, 52, 53, 54, 57, 58, 59, 60, 61, 64, 95, 113, 125, 133, 136, 137

B

Bangladesh-China-India-Myanmar Forum for Regional Cooperation (BCIM) xi, 8, 26, 36, 68, 71, 74

Beijing Consensus xiv, 66, 67, 72, 73, 75, 78

Belt Road Initiative xi, xiii, 14, 15, 16, 17, 19, 20, 21, 22, 47, 48, 49, 51, 53, 67, 68, 69, 70, 71

Boao Forum xi, 24, 53, 70, 77, 108, 136

Brazil-Russia-India-China-South Africa (BRICS) 15, 69, 71, 74, 133

C

China-Arab States Cooperation Forum (CASCF) 136

China-Arab States Expo 136

China-ASEAN financial cooperation 50

China-ASEAN Free Trade Agreement 50

China Development Bank 68, 83

China-Eurasia Expo 136

China International Fair for Investment and Trade 136

China Investment Corp 68

China-Pakistan Economic Corridor xi, 5, 8, 26, 68, 70, 129

China-Russia Expo 136

China-South Asia Expo 136

China's Silk Road 2, 23, 77, 96

China's single largest overseas project

Addis Ababa-Djibouti rail projects in East Africa 81

Mombasa-Nairobi railway in Kenya 81

Chinese Communist Party 17, 19

Chinese National Defense University 7

Chinese National Development and Reform Commission xi, 19

Conduct on Unalerted Encounters as Sea (CUES) 34

Conference on Interaction and Confidence-Building Measures in Asia (CICA) 136

Cooperation Afloat Readiness and Training 57

D

Deng Xiaoping 1, 15, 29

Department of Industrial Policy and Promotion xi, 90

DF-21D Anti-Ship Ballistic Missile 32

E

East Asia Summit (EAS) xi, 58

East China Sea xi, 34, 35, 114, 116, 121

Economic Cooperation, and Central Asia Regional Economic Coop-

eration (CAREC) 136

Euro-Asia Economic Forum 136

Export-Import Bank of China 68

F

Flying Geese Paradigm xi, 8, 12

Fujian Marine Economic Pilot Zone 138

G

Geographically Disadvantaged States 30

Global Maritime Nexus 26

Greater Mekong River Sub-regional Cooperation 20

Greater Mekong Sub-region (GMS) 136

Guangdong-Hong Kong-Macao Big Bay Area 138

Gurpreet S Khurana v, vii, 1, 46, 79

Gwadar port 8, 12, 70

H

H-6 aircraft 32

Haiyang Shiyou 981 34, 56

Haiyang Shiyou 982 53

Han Dynasty 1

Heartland 28

Horn of Africa 34

Hu Jintao 15

I

Indian Ocean Region xi, xiv, xv, 3, 4, 5, 6, 7, 28, 30, 34, 35, 40, 42, 74, 75

India's Spice Route 5

Indo-Pacific region xiii, 2, 3, 4, 6, 8, 9

Irene Chan v, vii, xiv, 47, 62

J

J-15 carrier borne aircraft 32

Jiang Zemin 15, 83

K

Kwa Chong Guan vi, vii, 99, 109

L

Li Keqiang 47, 50, 81, 95, 125, 139

Look East policy 26

Luyang III destroyers 32

Luyang I/II/III 31

M

MALUS Amphex 2014 57

Mao Zedong xiii, 1

Maritime Silk Road i, iii, v, vi, ix, x, xi, xiii, xiv, xv, 1, 2, 3, 4, 5, 6, 7, 8, 9, 10, 12, 14, 19, 21, 23, 24, 25, 26, 27, 28, 36, 47, 48, 49, 50, 51, 52, 53, 54, 56, 57, 58, 59, 60, 62, 63, 64, 66, 67, 68, 69, 70, 71, 72, 74, 75, 76, 77, 78, 79, 80, 81, 82, 83, 84, 85, 86, 87, 88, 89, 91, 92, 93, 94, 95, 96, 97, 99, 101, 102, 103, 104, 105, 106, 107, 108, 109, 111, 112, 113, 115, 116, 120, 121, 122, 125, 126, 128, 134, 137, 138, 141

ASEAN's Response 50

Background 126

China's Africa Push 80

Cooperation Mechanisms 135

Cooperation Priorities 129

Framework 128

History of an Idea 99

Principles 127

Regional Concerns 51

Master Plan on ASEAN Connectivity (MPAC) 50

Mausam projects xv, 5

Memorandum of Understanding xi

Mingjiang Li v, vii, 14

Mombasa-Nairobi railway in Kenya 81

N

Narendra Modi 74

National Defence University xi

National Maritime Foundation iv, vii, x, 11, 12, 79

Natural Resource Lands 28

Nazarbayev University, Kazakhstan 23

O

Oil and Natural Gas Corporation xi, 92

One Belt One Road v, ix, xi, xiii, 14, 24, 43, 47, 52, 67, 79, 80, 96, 122

Challenges for the BRI 20

P

P8A Poseidon Maritime Patrol aircraft 35

Paracel Islands 53, 56

People's Liberation Army (Navy) xi, 30

Pivot to the East 26

Project Mausam vi, xv, 11, 23, 99, 103, 111, 116, 118, 119, 120, 121, 122, 123

Q

Qianhai Cooperation Forum 136

R

Raghavendra Mishra v, vii, 23, 46

Rajaratnam School of International Studies x, 48

Rana Divyank Chaudhary v, vii, 66

Regional Perspectives on MSR

India 71

Pakistan 70

Sri Lanka 71

Responses of Countries on MSR

Indonesia 58

Malaysia 56

Singapore 57

Thailand 54

Vietnam 56

Rimland 28

S

Shanghai Cooperation Organization xi, 21, 133, 136

Silk Road Economic Belt vi, ix, xii, xiii, 14, 21, 23, 24, 47, 66, 67, 68, 69, 75, 77, 80, 93, 95, 98, 99, 108, 113, 125, 126, 128, 137, 141

South China Sea xi, 16, 35, 48, 49, 50, 52, 53, 54, 56, 57, 58, 59, 63, 64, 85, 99, 101, 102, 103, 104, 105, 106, 107, 114, 116, 121, 128

Sovremenny class destroyers 31

Spratly Islands 53, 56

Stockholm International Peace Research Institute xii, 33, 46

String of Pearls 6, 10, 11, 28, 45, 46, 62, 74

T

Tanzania Zambia Railway xii, 80

Tiananmen 15, 84

Trans-Pacific Partnership xii, 6

Type 022 (Houbei class) missile craft
31

Type 039A (Yuan) class SSK 31

Type 054A (Jiangkai II class) multi-
purpose frigates 31

Type 056 (Jiangdao class) missile corvettes 31

Type 071 (Yuzhao) 31

Type 072A (Yuting III) class amphibious assault ships 31

Type 093 (Shang) class SSN 31

Type 094 (Jin) class SSBN 31

W

Western China International Fair 136

Western Pacific Naval Symposium xii,
34

World Heritage 11, 56, 99, 116, 146

World Heritage List 116

X

Xi Jinping xiii, 1, 4, 8, 10, 12, 14, 17,
23, 43, 47, 60, 77, 81, 95, 99,
113, 125, 139

Z

Zhejiang Marine Economy Development Demonstration Zone 138

Zhoushan Archipelago New Area 138